My Unexpected Superpower

How Being Bipolar Got Me Ahead of Everyone Else

By Karina Schulz

The contents of this work, including, but not limited to, the accuracy of events, people, and places depicted; opinions expressed; permission to use previously published materials included; and any advice given or actions advocated are solely the responsibility of the author, who assumes all liability for said work and indemnifies the publisher against any claims stemming from publication of the work.

All Rights Reserved
Copyright © 2023 by Karina Schulz

No part of this book may be reproduced or transmitted, downloaded, distributed, reverse engineered, or stored in or introduced into any information storage and retrieval system, in any form or by any means, including photocopying and recording, whether electronic or mechanical, now known or hereinafter invented without permission in writing from the publisher.

Dorrance Publishing Co
585 Alpha Drive
Suite 103
Pittsburgh, PA 15238
Visit our website at *www.dorrancebookstore.com*

ISBN: 979-8-88683-314-0
eISBN: 979-8-88683-707-0

My Unexpected Superpower

How Being Bipolar
Got Me Ahead of Everyone Else

By Karina Schulz

*Dedicated to my dad,
who taught me that life is beautiful
and to never stop learning.*

CONTENTS

Introduction ix

1. What Is Bipolar? 1

2. My Childhood 11

3. Therapy 29

4. Taking Risks 47

5. Sex and Relationships 65

6. An Afterthought 91

7. Diets I've Tried 93

8. Proactivity 99

9. Being Bisexual 105

10. Work Life 109

11. How to Interact with Your Bipolar Friend or Family Member . . 119

Conclusion 125

INTRODUCTION

The day I figured out I had a superpower, I didn't categorize it as a superpower.

I knew I had one. When I was young, I dreamt of the day when someone would pop out of a bush, whisk me away, and tell me everything I was about to become. Not if but when. I knew I had a superpower. I was unstoppable! I. Was. Awesome. And above all, I knew I was different. I felt different things and couldn't explain it to other people in a clear way.

Was my superpower just now developing? Could I soon be able to time travel? Could I become invisible and eavesdrop on other people? Was I from a different planet? Would I be able to mind read and then change other people's opinions?! That last option was my favorite because I always felt people judging me, and if I could just take a swoop in and see what their thoughts were and make a few tweaks here and there, all would be great. Nothing big, just minor adjustments in my favor.

My superpower is being bipolar.

The day before my high school graduation, at 18 years old, my mom told me. She had wanted to hide it because she didn't want me judging other members of my family who clearly demonstrated some of the same symptoms. I thought and still think that's a stupid idea to hide the fact that your daughter is bipolar *from your daughter!*

After she told me though, everything made sense.

I've tried not to be too attached to labels in general, though.

A sales coach I had once said that my symptoms seemed more aligned with ADHD from what she could tell. That made me think that maybe I wasn't bipolar, but honestly, labels don't really matter. My crazy life is my crazy life, and that's that. Period. I identify as bipolar and that's that.

Couple my energy with my type "A" personality type and high "I" from the DISC profile, and you've got a bunch of avalanching ideas followed by bouts of dryness.

Turns out, the times when I thought I was on top of the world, I was just in a manic period. I love them. They are great. And over time, I've learned to channel my spike in energy towards positive projects and plans to create movement for activities and goals in my life.

As for the crazy people in my family, I thought they were whack. They are. But now that I know there was something hormonally misaligned, I stopped judging. Weird how that works.

It also turns out that people in public were, indeed, talking about me because I was talking—and still do always talk—to myself in public. I can't help it. I need to share my ideas with someone, and who is a better listener than the only other person who is 100 percent invested in making sure my project ideas get the full attention they deserve? Me. I'm the good listener. (Side note: Using masks during the pandemic was annoyingly useful for covering up the fact that I was talking to myself. All of a sudden, no one noticed).

I talk to myself at home, too. I'm hilarious. Sometimes I end up laughing so hard in my room by myself, my stomach hurts. I live with roommates, and they probably think that I'm watching some comedy show on Netflix. I've never told them I'm giving myself a comedy show. (Side note again: I do love comedy and stand-up shows, so it's possible that I actually am watching one of those as well).

Of course, there are the down moments, too. I can't deny it. They're horrible. Highly not recommended. (I know, I know—people with mental health disorders can't choose). But I'll get to that a little later and include tips I've used for myself to help overcome them.

Being bipolar, my thoughts are somewhat all over the place. So writing a book was extremely difficult. I started journaling with the intention to publish a book six years ago. And stopped five and a half years ago. My sprint lasted about six months. I kept getting distracted or highly invested in some other project I manifested. I sporadically got back into book writing on about four separate occasions since then.

It's funny because I can distinctly remember being around 12 years old and knowing that my interest level in something would fluctuate. I made a rule for myself: I could only proceed with a project if I was interested, then lost interest, and then got interested again. By reviving the interest, it confirmed that I *actually* was interested enough to complete whatever I had in mind. Things have changed a bit since then in terms of the analysis of my emotions, but as a child, I was already aware that something was different.

I have finally been able to compile a long enough thought to produce a long-form, coherent book by piecing together entries that I've made over the course of six years. The pieces were enough to complete one fourth of this manuscript. Having that as a base, I was able to build the rest in the span of about 3 months. By using the skeleton, I created a body and context.

Some chapters of the book my not flow as seamlessly from one topic to another as you'd like, but that's more how my brain works. Think of it as getting an insight into my thought process.

I want to demonstrate that it's okay to be different.

You should find and understand your personal needs to achieve the same, or better, results than your friends or family, who should also listen to their personal needs.

I compiled some of the most influencing events in my life

and decided to detail them individually in separate chapters. Each chapter allows you an insight into how I felt and how I dealt with certain events.

Whereas the subtitle of this book indicates that I will focus on bipolarity, this book can be for anyone with any mental illness.

I am passionate about helping other find what motivates them and how they can achieve their own goals, not someone else's. My purpose is to provide a first-hand account of how mental disorders are not or should not be inhibitors to achieving what you want. They can be the catalyst!

For people with other mental disorders, this book can be a base or inspiration to analyze your thought process from a different angle to see how you can best benefit in your personal and professional career. For those with no know or diagnosed mental disorder/s, this book can also serve to find more motivation by mindfully critiquing your situation at work, home, school or elsewhere.

Techniques I mention for mental organization, discipline and maturity are applicable to anyone at any age and from any walk of life.

Some stories I share are lighthearted and meant to cause chuckles or laughs. Others are hard to digest and even reading them back myself gives me shivers. Some of my stories have concrete endings while others are still active and present in my current life, meaning that the conclusions I arrive at and are discussed in this book may have altered since its publishing. You may think some of my reactions are exaggerated or unnecessary, which looking back was probably the case. But that's the past and this book is to give you an idea of how I got to where I am, based on the decisions that I made.

I ask that you stay curious. Question why I decided to act or not act on certain situations. My actions and reactions may be different than yours. You may agree or disagree with my decision, and that's okay. Your background may have influenced you to come to a different conclusion, and that's okay.

Overall, please enjoy reading and feel free to reach out to me personally should you want to challenge or discuss my mentality and choices.

CHAPTER 1

What Is Bipolar?

Also known as manic depression, bipolar disorder is a mental health condition that causes extreme mood swings and shifts in your energy and activity levels. There are two main types of bipolar disorder, and a third that combines the first two.
- *Bipolar I Disorder.* Contains both manic episodes (up to a week) and depressive episodes (two weeks or sometimes longer)
- *Bipolar II Disorder.* Predominantly just depressive episodes and sometimes manic, but *hypo*manic, meaning they are not as strong.

There is a third that I will not discuss just because it is not as common, and this is a book about how I handle it, not about the specifics of the disorder.

I have Bipolar I. I get both manic and depressive episodes, although I have only had two major depressive episodes in my life and a few minor ones.

To detail my feelings in the moment of a depressive episode, I found this excerpt from two months before I turned 19, when I was going through a difficult time:

> *If I were to commit suicide, I would jump off something high. Most likely a bridge over a busy freeway. [That gives me] the*

security that I if I didn't die from the impact of my landing, the cars would be driving too quickly to avoid my fractured body on the road, and I would die from a car blowing my body into a bloody pool in the middle of the lane. Now why am I thinking this? It terrorizes me just to have the thought. But lately it's been on my mind every day. Whenever something goes wrong, I feel like my surroundings would benefit from me not being there. After all, the world will only keep spinning and everyone else's lives will go on. People say that suicide hurts more people than you think. That it's not all about the victim, in this case me. It would hurt my parents, friends, etc. But in comparison to the amount of people in this world, so what if there's one less mouth to feed and a few sad hearts? How selfish of me is that? I'm not even human enough to consider the feelings of my own companions. But in reality that's exactly how I see everyone: companions. They're not friends nor caretakers but companions. And not close companions. They are people who are aware of my existence but would honestly rather hang out with someone else than with me. That's one of many reasons suicide seems like such a good solution.

I never actually attempted anything until a year later though. The first time I attempted suicide, I was alone in my college dorm apartment. I couldn't breathe. Add in the fact that I had the first and only full-on anxiety attack in my life and that coupled with depression. AND it was on my twentieth birthday…fun. I was alone in my room. All three of my roommates were in class.

    I had fully convinced myself that life should not go on. I was standing next to my twin XL unmade bed and had a nine-inch, sharpened Misen chef's knife held to my lower abdomen, which I had burrowed in my room, and was 100 percent ready for the plunge.

    I was crying. Obviously. I think it very unrealistic for a person on the edge of committing suicide to not have a face swelled to the size of a watermelon and be drenched in liquidy mucus, a nice mixture of salty tears and goopy, warm snot.

In addition to that, for some reason when I get extremely stressed and/or depressed, I get ear bleeds, so there was blood running from my ears leaving sporadically placed red splotches on my pillowcase and sheets. There was no blood close to the knife that was already in contact with my skin, innocently waiting for enough pressure to break the thin epidermis barrier between the crowded dorm room and the warm intestines still safe inside me.

How did I get out of it?

For whatever God-sent miracle (I'm not actually religious, but you get the point), I mustered up the will to call my friend. He happened to be my ex from high school, but we have stayed close friends to this day.

He stayed on the phone with me, listening to my weeping, crying pleas for life to end. My mind goes somewhat blank on the memory, so I couldn't tell you how he managed to convince me to get a grip, but he did.

I put the knife back in the kitchen cabinet all the way on the right, where all the other sharp, deadly knives were stored.

After calming down a bit more, I took an ice-cold shower. I HATE cold showers. But with the heat of my body and emotions in the moment, there was nothing better than getting berated with what seemed like ice pellets repeatedly.

I sat on the cold, plastic, and slightly yellow tinted floor of my shower. That's what weeping girls do in the movies, and it seemed like a movie moment. My hands rippled over the textured shower floor as my fingertips grew increasingly wrinkled. It helped a lot. I now like sitting on shower floors, chin tucked into my breastbone, creating a hollow space for me to breathe comfortably as the water washes around me and gently massages my back.

My roommates never came during my episode or during my almost hour-long shower. That was good because I wasn't close enough with them to share what was happening anyway.

I survived my twentieth birthday. The day after my twentieth birthday and first suicide attempt, I could officially accept my two decades of revolving around the sun.

However, later that week, I voluntarily enrolled myself in a mental health clinic with the understanding from my therapist that I could take part in an intensive OUTCARE patient program. Although the doctors attempted to get me into the in-patient program, my time there lasted only a few hours. I couldn't handle it. Mental health clinics, per my experience, do not do a good job of calming the patient down.

First, I had to get a referral from the university mental health center, which took a whole 15 minutes after I walked in, then it was off to the clinic.

It was a new building and was furnished like a spa retreat center; the kind you'd expect to find tucked away in a pocket in the Austrian Alps in the summer. Except this one was in the middle of Los Angeles. Beyond the lobby, furnished with decadent sofas, was a blue tiled fountain in a cozy, semi-outdoor courtyard filled with vibrant plants, curiously hypocritical of the drama the patients, including myself, were most likely experiencing.

By the time my turn came for my intake interview, I sat down across the room from the therapist and broke down again...which led her to inform me that she could legally not let me leave the facility. That wasn't my plan. I wanted out.

I just wanted the out-care patient program.

Honestly, the mental health system in the US needs a hefty upgrade. I got more anxious being there than being outside. On top of everything, I didn't want to explain to my mom what the charges for a mental clinic were on our next insurance bill. (I ended up telling her a few months later).

Being bipolar is difficult, but I've learned quite a lot over my few, but valuable, years here on Earth.

I've learned to harness my swings as a superpower rather than anything else. At first, it was because of necessity and needing to adapt to my environment and be successful no matter what; now, it is because I find joy in being able to come up with new solutions to problems that the run-of-the-mill person perhaps did not think of. I have an amazing superpower.

Before getting rolling, I wanted to share a few more entries from my journal around the same time as the first to present a more in-depth idea of what was happening in my mind.

Here are two more excerpts from my journal:

Excerpt 1:

There were times when the worst question was "How are you?"

I had no answer.
I couldn't even muster up am "I'm fine" to a close friend.
I wasn't fine.
I was hurting but the pain, it was locked away.
Yet everyone had the password to get in.

There were times when I couldn't answer the question "How are you?" without breaking into tears. There was no "good" or "fine" or even a simple "stressed." I wanted to kill myself. I did not want to continue to live on this planet. I did not see happiness at the end of any tunnel. I couldn't muster up a simple answer because it was too hidden. I pushed my feelings away so much. I had kept them locked in and under so much control for so long that it was impossible to continue. Answering and saying

I was bad or depressed only led to tears.

Once I called my stepdad. After a few minutes of small talk, he stopped and asked how I was doing. I'm not sure he even noticed my pause or the change in my voice when responding. I said I was stressed and sad. He didn't notice any difference in my voice.

Excerpt 2:

I do not enjoy being in my head right now. I want to be able to see and feel what other people see and feel. It all seems so much more liberating in other people's minds. There is no clutter there. No obsessing over unnecessary things. There is no repetitive analysis. There is no longing for a better situation. There is no feeling out of connection with your body.

There is happiness. There is peace and understanding. Out there, somewhere. Outside my head lies a place where all the pieces fit and an extra one didn't make its way into the box only to be deemed useless.

Reading my journal entries is hard. I've been sitting in front of my computer now for quite some time rereading them back. There's so much that has changed but also so much has stayed the same.

In the first entry, I can still remember sitting in my dorm room twin XL bed freshman year of college and having my stepdad on the phone during that specific conversation. I was drained after such a simple catch-up call.

I really felt that there was nothing else that I could provide to anyone on this planet.

In the second entry, I mention having an extra puzzle piece put in a box that was then rendered useless. Although I didn't think much of the metaphor at the time of writing, looking back I feel how peculiar of a comparison it was to make.

Usually, I've read that people feel they are missing pieces or not understanding something because information is missing. In my case, I felt I had *too much*. There were *too many emotions* and *too many thoughts* running through my head that overwhelmed me.

Instead of having a puzzle with a few blank spaces, I had a completed board with random pieces on the side that no one knew what to do with, and no one could interpret where the pieces would even go because the blurry and partial image seen was not decipherable.

As time went on, I realized that having those extra pieces of information helped me. I still feel I have extra pieces. Those now contribute to my superpower.

Yes, I'm more emotional. But being cognizant of it meant that I gave myself the space to work through those emotions, and get to know my triggers and reactions sooner than most people. Personally, this means that I became more aware of other people's reactions and therefore could also be a more supportive friend or companion when I was needed. Professionally, there is a new trend in showing a high emotional IQ, also known as EQ (emotional quotient). Recruiters or hiring managers will not just look for an individual who can complete certain tasks but also one who can interact well with others and overcome difficulties in his or her own production with a certain level of emotional maturity.

In the second journal entry, I also mention over analyzing everything. Whereas not beneficial in every situation, channeling my analytic side on the right projects helps me to foresee different outcomes based on different paths that I could take.

By having gone through all these hoops at the beginning of my professional career, I bypassed a huge percentage of people who all "had things in order."

Overall, it's a good exercise to reread your thoughts from the past. If you haven't kept a journal, maybe just a reflection on everything you've done is sufficient.

Through rereading my thoughts, I can see how far I've come and now interpret everything as a positive. My superpower. Was I emotional? Yes. And I still am. I give myself the space to emote and then get back on track.

I can see how far I've come but also see that there is so much more I have to learn.

But now, back to information about bipolarity.

Bipolar is a mental condition characterized by emotional highs and lows. The peaks and troughs typically go hand-in-hand with energy levels and metabolic rates. During certain points in the cycle, high levels of energy and countless new project ideas can be sustained for days at a time. And sometimes it means just two to three hours of sleep without eating.

Other times, four hours of working seems like an eternity, and I can't stop eating.

Bipolarity can be *intense*, to say the least.

There are countless stigmas associated with bipolar disorder. However, the majority of the time, a person with bipolar disorder is in a neutral, or non-episodic state. Unfortunately, others will characterize a bipolar person based on his or her episodes. Some critiques include: being crazy, being anti-social, being overly energetic, being aggressive, being impulsive, and more.

That doesn't mean that a bipolar person can't get work done, and very well.

Throughout this book, I will detail stories from my life where being bipolar has actually come to my benefit. At the moment, I may not have registered it as such, but as time goes on and I look back, I was actually a step ahead of most other people.

Every day, I advance more towards learning how to interpret my emotions and use them as a positive rather than a negative. My purpose is to show others that no matter what emotional cards they were dealt at birth or acquired over the span of their life, they can slowly but surely flip the deck around and turn it into a superpower. Everyone can achieve a goal, just not using the same route as others.

Here are a few stories about my successes and failures! I hope you enjoy them and are able to gain some insight into what it's like to be bipolar and expand the lessons to your own life. You also have a superpower!

CHAPTER 2

My Childhood

My parents got divorced when I was three years old. According to anyone in the family you would ask, it is because my paternal grandmother told my dad "this woman is not good enough."

My mom was too strict, too restrictive, too low-class, or whatever else my grandmother invented to convince my dad that she was not perfect for him. My dad, being the first born and oldest son to a traditional Latina mom, was heavily influenced and spoiled by my grandmother. He did essentially everything that she wanted.

The Christmas and New Year's time of the turn of the millennium, my dad vacationed in Peru by himself, leaving my mom and me by ourselves in San Diego. Low and behold, after two weeks of what I can only imagine consisted of intensive lectures from my grandmother, my dad came back and filed for divorce.

My mom was devastated, and according to her, I cried and pleaded for Daddy to come home some nights. In a way, I can't complain about all this having happened when I was so young because I can't remember anything. I definitely developed some sort of commitment issues, which has translated into tension in romantic relationships and led to the tendency to flee, but besides that, growing up with just one parent was pretty normal for me.

I didn't register it at the time, but looking back, I can see how incredibly strong my mother had to be in those first years by herself. She had a three-year-old that needed to be dropped off at daycare at

6:00 in the morning and picked up at 6:00 PM because she had to run to work to be able to support the household. She did not yet own a house or condo, so we also moved from apartment to apartment frequently. By the time I was seven, I had lived in five different apartments.

My mom knew that the only way that I would get ahead of the game is to get a good education. Not once did my mom *ever* hesitate to invest in an experience that would contribute directly to my education. I'm not exactly sure how she did it, but I'm nothing but extremely grateful for the emphasis that she showed.

I went to a Montessori pre-school and then to a German-immersion charter school from kindergarten to eighth grade, which acted more like a public school because it still received some funding from the San Diego City School District although there were fundraising events to support more in-depth programs.

Although we were tight on money and my mom didn't make much more than minimum wage, and wasn't a US citizen yet, she managed to fund all the education programs that helped to stimulate my love for lifelong learning.

For example, when I was 12, I participated in an exchange program in Germany. I was hosted by a German family in Giessen, a small town close to Frankfurt. Then my assigned exchange student, Anna, who was one year older than me, came and lived with us in San Diego. We went to each other's school classes and immersed ourselves in each other's cultures. I went horseback riding and picnicking with Anna's family and Anna came to the beach and Belmont Park with me.

My mom also managed to fund my sports fees. I got into competitive cheerleading, which is not at all a budget sport—$900 just to get started with the basics of the uniform. Everything "from bow to toe," as a cheerleader would say and then the bag, pom-poms, trips, and competition fees on top of that.

Above all, she did what she could to make sure I got the most exposure possible to different languages, extracurricular activities, distinct cultures, and a good education. My mom is truly an outstanding woman and has given so much of her life to ensure that I, her daughter, had all the tools necessary to flourish and be in a better situation than she was.

Having all this diversified education goes in line with being bipolar. I learned to be curious and that taking on a new path is alright.

I poke my head into a lot of things that maybe I shouldn't, just for the experience. Some events are more directly related to bipolar than not.

Once while touring catacombs in Rome, I touched the bones. They told us not to because they were human bones and couldn't handle the natural human grease from my fingers. I touched it anyway. TBD on if they are actually human bones or not.

I also sign up for some random courses or take on projects because I think they are awesome at the moment.

I once thought I would join the circus, so I spent days researching terminology and techniques for getting into the circus. I ended up never even applying.

Then I thought I would be an equestrian star. I took a few classes in Austria. I love horses, but the sport was way too expensive to maintain myself.

Another time, I thought it would be cool to ride camels in the Sahara, so I bought a ticket to Morocco and a month later was knee-deep in burning hot sand and covered with a cloth face shield to block out the sandstorm that whipped around my tour group and me on our way on camel back from Merzouga towards the Moroccan-Algerian border. Random trip to Africa: check. (And no, I never got to Casablanca, which is definitely the most known city there).

Bipolar disorder manifests itself differently in children than it does in adults. With children, swings are typically closer together and not as strong. A manic episode can come directly after a depressive episode that only lasted a week.

Children in general are still learning how to deal with emotions, and their brains are still developing the correct neuronal pathways to correctly interpret what they are feeling and, more importantly, how to react to outside stimulants.

Bipolar disorder in adults is manifested in longer waves. A depressive period will last a few weeks longer followed by a period of calmness, which is neither manic nor depressive. Then a manic episode will hit but typically isn't registered by others as such because it is a high energy period that can typically be caused by some good news. So, others may see it as a natural reaction to the news rather than a symptom of being bipolar.

I can attest that this is similar to what happened to me.

As a teenager, I often thought that I was a hypochondriac because I was constantly feeling something different. Surprise! I was. I spent countless nights on google confirming that I was a hypochondriac, which then changed later on.

I started writing a journal, but then three months, later I stopped. Then I started again a year later, then stopped. I get really into it for a while but don't see the benefit long-term. And like that in cycles. You can argue that this is pretty normal for non-bipolar individuals as well, but that's up for interpretation.

As a teenager, I spent multiple nights on the floor in my bedroom at night crying for no particular reason. Sometimes, I would stay up and sit in my closet with the door closed because it was comfortable and warm. Closing the door to my closet created a cozy environment where I could think.

Once I got caught texting until 1:00 AM, and my mom said that was unacceptable. I'm not sure why. I still got perfect grades. My mom involved my dad, who really didn't care. He told me privately that it didn't matter. As long as I was still disciplined enough to get my work done and not do drugs, the time I went to bed didn't matter to him.

She threatened to call Verizon and open up every text message that was sent at that time. Obviously, I freaked. I hadn't been sending any inappropriate messages about anything scandalous, but why was she getting involved? Clearly there was no privacy. I was furious. From my perspective, she thought I was the most irresponsible child. I think we can all agree that there are worse things than sending late text messages.

From leadership books I had read when I was younger, I already was familiar with the idea of "*show* people the way you want to be treated." I was an overachieving kid with no alcohol, drug, or other addiction problems. I gave her space and wanted some as well. I didn't know how to communicate that to her as a teenager.

Another time while in college, she came to visit me, and while I was in the bathroom, she snooped through my drawers to find my hidden medicine container of lithium, the drug typically used for bipolar. The university mental health clinic prescribed it to me to try. I didn't tell my mom and was absolutely furious she would invade my privacy. Again, top university, passing all my classes. Why was she purposely looking for something I was doing wrong?

Now that I've lived by myself for years, my method is just not sharing details about pretty much anything with her because I have set an emotional limit. I know I will get angry if I cross on purpose, so I just avoid it all together.

As an adult, I take the mature natural step backwards when I see my emotions are starting to get out of hand and question if there is a valid reason to be feeling the way I am feeling at that moment.

If there is no particular reason for me to be extremely happy or extremely sad, then I am already halfway through getting over it. I give myself the space I need to either cry for no reason or to bounce off the walls without critique and then flip the page and continue. If I need to take a weekend out of the city to completely disconnect, then I do that in order to breathe and reconvene with myself. Otherwise, I have learned to use my emotional tools that help me alter the way I react externally to what I am feeling internally.

How can all of this prove I have a superpower?

Because I can now have fully informed and personalized conversations with almost anyone. I have things in common with so many more people. I am a wealthy source of information for those who perhaps want to try something new because of my various experiences. For example, what is it like to pee in the desert? Weird. It's weird. And they serve hot, boiling hot, food because, to the native Saharans, increasing your body temperature as close to the outside temperature creates a lesser difference, so you don't actually feel the heat as much. (I still wanted ice cold water though).

My superpower, being bipolar, primed me at a younger age than most, to figure my shit out.

* * *

Now, on to the rest of my family.

My paternal family is whack. Each member is a little bit weird or messed up in his or her own special way. I love each one. Honestly, with my whole heart. My maternal family I don't have much connection with.

My paternal family is Latino and follows lots of typical stereotypes about other Latin families.

My grandmother tries to run the show. She's a typical Latina mother who wants to keep all her chicks in her nest for ever and ever. She gossips all the time but then says that being kind to others is key.

I love her very much, and she's shown me an insurmountable number of lesson that I will never forget, but there's definitely the manipulative side.

She never understood what it meant to be bisexual, which is how I identify, so we basically ignore the topic of romance all together.

She claims to not be a feminist because women are better than men and feminism is about equality. So screw equality.

She's never once given me a Christmas or a birthday present. And she's not the type to hug much. In that aspect, she's different from other warm, loving Latina grandmothers.

She's poised and always ready to listen to how I'm feeling and comment on my actions or thoughts.

However, she also never fails to say how much she loves and cares for me. She wants to see me shine.

My grandmother is a great judge of character. Judgy in general, yes, also. But when I have gone to ask for specific advice on a situation, she lets me explain the entire situation and then gives a detailed opinion on what she suggests is the best next step by taking into consideration my past and my personality type:

"You are too hyper for a project as mundane as that one."

Or:

"That is something 100 percent up your alley. Continue forward and make as many connections and learn as much as you possibly can from the experience."

She then will use specific examples to back up her theory:

"Remember when you moved to Peru in 2016 and immediately got involved in social communities? That shows your independence and ability to create connections in cross-cultural situations and demonstrates that you can be flexible with your surroundings. Therefore, continue on X path."

I loved that response.

We don't talk as much as we probably should. I admit that it's my fault. But when we talk it goes on for hours. And she's always ready to listen with an open ear. I love her very much and appreciate her voice in my decision-making process.

Then there's my dad: Ohhhh, my dad. He's definitely the person I'm closest to out of the whole bunch. Aunts, uncles, cousins, and the extended family who no one can ever remember correctly. I'm closer to my dad than I am my mom, although I love them both.

My dad is my biggest influence and role model. I love him

so much. My dad is also crazy. The last time I visited him in Vegas, he basically chased a girl down the sidewalk because he wanted to know what she was listening to. She had earbuds in, and that was just too confusing for him.

I used to hold him back a lot. I would get so embarrassed. How could I not?! Seeing a 68-year-old man bullet down a sidewalk after a young, probably 20-something-year-old girl is not a comfortable situation. In fact, many would call the police. From experience, I know that would be no use, so I've learned to live with and even laugh at most situations. At least, the ones that do not cause harm physically or emotionally to others.

One time in high school he showed up on campus and crouched down by the window of my classroom. One classmate shouted out to the class, "There is a man looking through the window!"

I ran out and pulled him away, dreading the walk back into the room.

My dad and I can also get into the most intense fights about absolutely nothing important. Once in Peru, we started yelling—really YELLING—at each other in a vegan restaurant in Miraflores, an upscale neighborhood in Lima.

What was the fight about? Social classes.

At this point, I had been living in Peru for a few months already. In order to make friends, I had started attending LGBT groups and going to LGBT nightclubs. My social bubbles started to grow.

Whereas the US has extreme income, racial, and gender inequality, you can't always tell by looking at someone or hearing how they speak if they belong to a certain socio-economic class or not. To be fair, I also went to an inner-city public high school where that wouldn't at all be claimed to source from high-income families. So, being the most fancy, uptight or anything related to high-class wasn't on my radar.

In Peru, I was making friends, and I liked that.

My father did not like the friends that I was hanging out with.

None of the friends I had were alcoholics, drug addicts, not studious, or any of the other major turn-offs to parents trying to protect their children.

The only thing my dad did not like was that they were not born into the same socio-economic class of his family. In Peru, his family was quite well off in comparison to others.

That's where the discussion started.

"Hanging out with those people is a waste of time!" he yelled at me.

"How?! They are emotionally there for me and treat me well!" I yelled back.

The conversation went on. Everyone in the restaurant was looking at us. At this point, I didn't care. I couldn't believe my dad was being so shallow with people he had never had a full-on conversation with and was refusing to even try to have a conversation with.

I stood my ground, and he stood his.

We paid and fought during the entire walk back to my grandma's house. I COULD NOT believe him.

But right when we got through the front door and into his office, everything changed.

My dad looked me in the eyes and took a deep inhale. This automatically made me inhale deeply as well.

He closed his eyes. I followed.

Another breath.

"Despite our differences of opinion, I love you," he said.

I paused.

"I love you, too."

We hugged. A big, warm, loving hug.

And this is where I learned. We had differences of opinion. However, just because of the differences, he wasn't actually trying to change what I did. He never said to stop hanging out with those people, he just voiced what he thought about the situation.

So what's the point? Well, you can have differences with someone but still get along, and that's totally fine.

A similar situation came up a few years later when the 2016 presidential election of Trump vs. Hillary Clinton took over the news and any conversation.

At this point, my dad was already a naturalized US citizen, meaning he could vote in the US elections.

He supported Trump. I did not.

We were both extremely set in our opinions.

Again, there were arguments that ended in yelling. This time, thankfully, in private. There was also madly rushing out of rooms without letting the other person finish and slamming doors.

Honestly, not the way to go.

There really wasn't any point to it.

I loved and love everything else about my dad.

Eventually, we came to the same conclusion. Deep breath in, hug, love each other. Love and being kind. That's the solution.

The most frequent occurrence that embarrasses me to this day is that he yells at everyone. This is a combination of him having a naturally very loud voice, and in Peru, service jobs are not looked at the same way as in the States. One way is not better than the other, just different, but a cultural integration needs to take place in order to act correctly in each society.

In Peru, for example, when not in tourist areas, which have adopted a more American style service, a waiter at a restaurant will not come up and ask you every five minutes if you are doing alright. If you drop a fork on the floor, need a new napkin, or want to order something else, then you raise your hand and wave down the waiter. If they don't see you, then you say "excuse me" to be heard.

In the States, you typically wait to be seated, then wait to be attended and wait for the check.

Combining my dad's Peruvian habits with his naturally loud

voice, what you get is a man screaming halfway across a loud restaurant in downtown San Francisco that he needs more sauce for his fish and an extra side of rice.

It's freaking embarrassing.

Whereas I frequently get embarrassed by him and feel I have to discipline him, me being his daughter, I still couldn't be prouder.

He's extremely successful and has never failed to support me when I need it.

I can call him crying, and he'll listen; or call him laughing, and he'll laugh with me. When I have a problem, he'll never say, "It'll be alright." Instead, he says, "Okay, this is a problem. You can't get to your goal using the path you intended to. So adjust your path. Let's make a new plan." And then he'll work through a new idea with me.

I can tell my dad all my crazy plans because he understands what it's like to not be able to control ideas.

Above all, he shows me love, and he always has, even though he divorced my mom when I was three years old and moved out of the city.

The thing is, I get it now. Since I figured out more about being bipolar, I understand the need to pick up and move. I understand being bored. And I understand being EXTREMELY interested in something one day and not the next.

I can share my dream boards or New Year's resolutions with him. He reads all my documents, and he always asks for more detail. And he holds me accountable.

One time, I told him how much I missed horseback riding and how I wanted to do it again. He told me that I wasn't allowed to call him until I was with horses.

That forced me to research where I could find horse stables in Lima, an extremely densely populated urban, not at all horse-friendly city.

I found one an hour out of the city.

When I went, I couldn't find the entrance, and no one would answer my calls. I walked for an hour before giving up and starting my walk back. But my dad's voice rang inside me and told me to go back. I made the 20-minute trek back from what I had already walked away. On my way back, I finally got a call back from the stable owner. She had been busy and couldn't answer the phone.

As soon as I got back, the gates were opened for me.

Had I not turned around, I would've already flagged down a taxi and been on my way home.

I video-called my dad through WhatsApp, and instead of "Hi," he said, "Are you with horses?" I was.

When I visit my dad, in whatever city he happens to live in at the time, we follow a similar routine. I don't learn from what he says to me; I learn from what he shows me. He shows me dedication and motivation.

He wakes up at 3:00 AM (that's a bit over the top for me). I wake up between 5 and 6 AM. We sit down, and until 10:00 AM, we are completely quiet, working. That is our collective but separate "me time." We spend time together comfortably, each working on his or her own project and advancing the ideas that we want to advance.

Around 10:00 AM, we start with basic chat of what our plans are for the day and which projects we will be working on. Similar to hiring a coach, having someone else to be accountable to helps ensure that you focus. He once shared his plans about concreting a choice on which yearly memberships to join and which trips to plan while also advancing his work projects. I shared that I would finish the entire manuscript draft of the book you are currently reading by the end of the week, dedicating myself to writing 3,000 words per day.

He did it. And I did it.

My dad gives me the confidence to be me, superpower and all. We both know the power of focus and the power of letting the mind run when it needs to run. Play is necessary. And so is work.

My dad is there for me when I'm down and when I'm up. No conditional love whatsoever.

The relationship I have with my mom is quite different.

She's steadier but not as much of a go-getter as my dad.

That in no way makes her less important; she's just different, and I'm extremely thankful for having had her in my life growing up.

My mom constantly told me that I was able to do whatever I wanted in life, and she was the biggest catalyst in making sure that I got the absolute best education I possibly could for our income level. (We were not in the market for being a private-school family).

My mom raised me as a single parent and still managed to save enough money to buy her own condo when I was nine years old. That was big because before, it seemed as if we were moving from one apartment building to the next for quite some time.

She also taught me the importance of creating a loving environment. As she started dating my stepdad, she ensured that I was comfortable every step of the way (something my dad did not do with his various girlfriends over the span of my life).

I had an active voice in everything that happened. Although I would imagine lots of therapists or divorced couples would praise a single mother for first taking care of her own happiness in her love life, my mom understood that I was also going to be living in the house with *both of* them. This man was going to take me to school and eat meals with us. I needed to get along with him as much as she did. Had she created a tense environment, I would have resented her and her new husband my whole life.

She asked me if I felt comfortable enough for her to marry him, and I said yes.

My mom is generally a bubbly, happy go-lucky, ridiculously talkative person. She is happy the way she lives her life and doesn't try to interfere with the lives of others, besides critiquing the people she sees on reality TV shows.

Although not as understanding of my superpower, my mom showed me love, which was extremely important as well.

Continuing on with the family…

My paternal grandfather grew up as an elite in Prague in the early twentieth century. He spent his days in one of the more than 20 rooms of his castle reading and studying, or he would take a 10-minute stroll to the horse stables out back to ride through the then lush forestry of Czechoslovakia, now Slovakia and the Czech Republic.

According to my uncle, the Schulz family in Prague was the first to own a microwave and a television set. Whereas I can't say this is completely confirmed, it's nice to think that I came from some sort of royalty.

"My grandfather owned a castle in Europe." Honestly not a bad way for me to start a conversation.

"My grandfather escaped the Russians." Also, an intriguing way to start a conversation and definitely beads higher curiosity for an explanation.

My paternal grandfather escaped communist Prague, Czechoslovakia (before the country divided into the Czech Republic and Slovakia), after World War I. He hopped on a boat in France due south, crossing the Atlantic Ocean. His first stop was in Curazao, just above the northern tip of Venezuela, in the Caribbean.

There, he received a warm welcome into Latin America. However, he continued his journey until he arrived at the port of El Callao, a municipality bordering Lima, the capital of Peru.

As the story goes, per his fleeing status, he was given exactly $8 US dollars upon offboarding to get situated in Peru. There was no family inheritance, as his family's hometown, savings, and belongings were now government-owned. Either the Russians or the Germans took everything his family had. (It's been told that he and his family members freaked out every time there was an earthquake in Lima because it resembled the shaking that they felt three times in Prague when foreign military armed vessels came storming through the city to take control, again.)

Lucky for my grandfather, he knew that the best aspect that would get him through tough times was a good education. What he could carry in his head was more than anyone could ever give him physically.

In Europe, he had the fortunate background of a high-class education in Prague and had then studied law in France.

Yes, he was definitely privileged in that sense; however, after the Soviets came in, he had lost absolutely everything: home, money, credibility, and most importantly, ability to return to his family.

In Peru, he showed up to a networking group and hit the ground running—without speaking a lick of Spanish. He started interacting with people in Spanish only, the little he knew, and grew his network and knowledge day after day.

With one cent to his name, he started growing his empire.

He started studying law in Peru and started practicing. Through the initial networking group that he showed up to, he met my grandmother.

Although my grandmother admits to never before having been attracted to "white men," he stole her heart, and two years later, they were married.

My grandfather ended up carrying such a high post in his job that he was able to buy a huge house and plot of land in what would become the most important neighborhood of Lima. He instilled in his children the importance of first educating yourself.

My grandmother came from a numerous family in the center of Lima where money was extremely tight from day one.

Her family reused napkins (even if there were lipstick stains on one side), only designated one fruit to each kid daily (no doubles, because that's a waste), bought the cheapest bread available, and didn't allow for seconds at dinner; extra food was to be used for the next family meal.

However, similar in mentality to my grandfather's upbringing, my grandmother valued education over anything else.

Everyone's income (all children, parents, and other family members in the house) was pooled into one bucket and then redistributed to each member as needed. For example, my grandmother was accepted for a study abroad program in Chile but wouldn't have been able to afford it herself. Because of her mother's tedious control over family finances, my grandmother was able to go to Chile, fully funded by the family's *combined* income.

My grandmother grew and grew and eventually got into politics.

She worked alongside the Peruvian congress and to this day is invited to events with the president and the rest of the governing houses in Peru.

Step by step, she grew by educating herself.

Both my grandmother and grandfather created a household that prioritized learning, reading, and educating yourself over everything so that you can get ahead.

By the time my dad got to his early and mid-thirties, Peru had shifted.

The Peruvian economy experienced hyperinflation, a communist government, and social instability. Alberto Fujimori was president and was leading the country through a downward spiral.

At this point, my dad now had a wife and two daughters, a three-year-old and a six-year-old, in Lima. But the situation was getting tougher with each passing day.

Finally, he and three of his siblings decided to work together and moved to the United States in hopes of a more lucrative future.

My dad's wife at the time did not agree that moving away from her family was the correct thing to do, much less with two young children in tow. My dad moved anyway, leaving his two daughters and wife in Peru.

My father eventually got a divorce, married my mom, and had me.

Three of the four siblings who moved to the States initially still live there and have found their own forms of success and happiness.

Generation after generation, my family has had to rebuild wealth, connections, and a name for itself.

My mother when she moved to the United States did not speak a lick of English, but she was determined.

My grandfather, a native Czechoslovakian, after having moved to Peru from France to escape the invading Russians, had to learn Spanish and create a name for himself in a foreign country in order to support his new wife and quickly bore seven children over the proceeding 10 years after arriving in Lima.

My father and his siblings, my aunts and uncles, fled communist Peru under Fujimori to land in the United States without knowing even how to ask where the bathroom was in English. Good luck trying to get an apartment under those circumstances.

Everyone took what they had, including an extremely optimistic attitude, and grew from there.

I was never given much monetarily, nor will I have much to inherit (as of right now—who knows what will happen in the future?), but I was given a stellar philosophy on education and a drive to continue forward. The instillation of a go-getter and positive attitude towards the future also helps when my bipolar leads me down a different path.

How does my superpower come into play here? Well, I don't fear instant change as much as others. If I need to adapt emotionally or otherwise, I do it as quickly as possible without hesitation.

The mental foundation and deterministic attitude I was shown as a child, made me aware that I need to use what I have, my superpower, to my benefit and grow from there.

My whole family, although each individual has his or her peculiarities, has shown me love. I am undeniably grateful for that because dealing with bipolar can definitely be difficult at times and having a support crew can make the rough times not as rough.

CHAPTER 3

Therapy

Therapy is alleviating.

I started seeing a therapist the month after writing the journal entries from the first chapter. My first meeting with her was nothing less than AMAZING and a pivotal moment in my life when I realized there was someone who could talk me through my own thoughts. I do not know how I got so lucky to have such an exceptional therapist on the first try. I have since realized that does not happen to others. It takes various tries to match with a therapist.

Finding a therapist is like online dating. You have to make appointments with a few, meet with them a couple of times, and get a feeling for how they run their sessions and see if you "vibe" with them or not.

Finding a therapist you like is ridiculously hard.

Since I could not afford to pay $200 to $250 out of pocket once per week for hourly sessions (either online or in-person), I clearly was only looking for therapists who would take my insurance. That limited my search even more.

I was under my mom's health insurance from Scripps Hospital in San Diego. The mental health coverage offered was for therapists in our region. Ergo, in our registered zip code. I went to college at University of Southern California, in Los Angeles—a good 200 miles from my zip code.

However, there was an insurance extension that I was able to tap into that allowed me to source a limited number of therapists in the USC area. The selection was not great. Apart from almost every therapist already being fully booked (great to know that so many other people in the States need help), traffic in LA and not having a car impeded my search further to offices I could either walk or bus to.

One time I ended up with a therapist from a foreign country I won't mention as to not call it out. The fact that she was foreign, though, is an important aspect to the story. She was horrible. One time I overheard her with the patient before me. They were arguing. The therapist literally didn't let her patient have her own thoughts and emotions.

When my turn came, the same thing happened.

I told her I wanted to move to Peru after college. My paternal family is Peruvian; I had been there multiple times and didn't want to live in the land of the "free" anymore. I had known this for as long as I can remember.

Her opinion? (Not that her opinion was supposed to matter anyway, but....). No. I couldn't go. I had to stay. It was a stupid idea to go to Peru because the income level in Peru was lower than in the United States. Long live the red, white, and blue. As a foreigner, she thought it strictly her place to inform me of the negative aspects of moving to the third world. She gave me a lecture on all the opportunities she had gained after having moved to the States. Good for her. My life is different.

According to her, in the third world, the people are rude, there is no job growth, no education. Just horrible.

Spoiler: I moved to Peru anyway, and it was one of the best professional decisions I could have made in my life, so far... More on that later.

After ranting to my roommate about how bad my therapist was, I realized I needed therapy for my therapy. She was booted.

Another time I found a therapist located in San Diego who did virtual sessions.

I scheduled my first online session.

Outside therapy, no one has ever mentioned that word "anxiety" as many times in one hour as she did. Just being with her made me more anxious.

Then she started telling me stories about what her other bipolar patients and friends had done.

"One time, my friend decided at midnight that she needed to repaint the kitchen. Now she has a half green kitchen."

"One of my ex-military patients was so happy with therapy that she thought she should be a therapist. She enrolled in classes and bought books, only to drop the idea three months later."

As relatable as that last anecdote is to me, I really didn't want to be with a therapist who would openly share my intimate stories and life experiences with her other patients.

Booted. And I never paid the session fee that was invoiced to me later.

Not apologizing.

I saw a few other therapists but got frustrated. I went a few years without therapy.

I had given up.

What had made my first therapist so great was her ability to listen. To *really* listen. She would even allow for a llloonnnggg break after I spoke before she started talking. In my mind, she was ensuring that there wasn't anything else I wanted to add on before she asked a question or touched on a new topic.

I cried during almost every session I had with her and came out of her office feeling lifted. I'd compare this to the freeing feeling of being on cocaine, but I've never snorted, so I wouldn't know. Her therapy sessions gave me something along the lines of the descriptors I know of cocaine highs.

On the multiple times I confessed to having another suicidal dream or thought, we would work through the details of it to find manageable solutions. Probably per guidelines, she would always ask if I had consciously thought-out plans. That's a tell-tale sign that your patient is close to acting.

I brought her the journal entry that I shared in the first chapter and read it to her out loud.

"Can I share some data with you about people who jump off bridges?" she asked.

"Of course," I responded, eager to change my despair.

"The few people who have survived high falls, typically into lakes or rivers, always confess that they regretted the jump on the way down. A solution for people contemplating a fatal jump is to engage in some sort of simulation, for example skydiving or bungee jumping."

Apparently, by simulating the action of falling, you can get a feel for what it would be like to actually fall.

I have since gone skydiving in Las Vegas, approximately 40 minutes from the strip. It wasn't scenic at all, but somewhat adrenaline-inducing. Then I went bungee jumping in Azuza, California, at a place called "Bridge to Nowhere." There is a two-hour hike to get in, and then, you guessed it, a bridge that leads to nowhere... Skydiving wasn't so scary. Bungee jumping scared the fucking sanity right back into me.

The rocks coming at my face at an acceleration of -9.8 meters per second was not comforting.

Wanting to commit suicide by jumping? Yeah, no thanks. Problem solved.

Another time I confessed my knife-to-stomach suicide attempt.

My therapist explained that during those intense emotional times, it's necessary for our brain to somehow find a way to release happy, or healing, hormones. If I were to have cut, there would have been an increase in hormones that would have swept in to help heal the cut. It feels sort of like a "high." This is one reason people who cut frequently repeat in future occasions. There actually is a high.

(In no way am I saying you should actually self-harm.)

Thankfully, there is a way around this.

My wonderful therapist got right to the point: "You're trying to inflict pain on yourself. You can achieve a similar feeling without it being life-threatening."

"Um, sorry, what?"

"Take two ice cubes and hold one in each hand. Hold them as tight as you can and don't let go until you can't feel your hands. Your body will react the same way, by spiking all the biological mechanisms it can to heal the area. You will get a rush, get pushed out of your depressive moment, and not have broken any skin in the process."

Thinking I need self-harm to be life threatening? No need. Problem solved.

She had a way of not being scared of the deepest emotions. She went straight for them.

I have since taken on her creative and no-nonsense way of thinking to solve some emotional crises myself.

I got that same "feel-good" head rush after getting waxed once. Of course, after the initial pain died down. And waxing doesn't break any skin. No problems! And it's a little bit of self-care as the cherry on top.

Going hard at the gym also provides the same high.

As mentioned, I hate the cold and cold showers, so no, I do not use the supposedly energy-boosting cold shower technique. I realized though, that I enjoy taking warm showers or being surrounded by warm water in general. I use boiling hot showers to simulate a comforting environment. It feels like a giant hug and I like that. Being in the shower also means that I am not on my phone, computer, or interacting with anyone else, which means no distractions. It is strictly a time for me.

Probably the most difficult solution to try is literally sitting and telling myself, "It's just your hormones; you don't actually want to commit suicide," and repeating that as a mantra until I either fall asleep or force myself to go out and plan an activity with a friend.

I've used this creative mindset to overcome other types of stressful situations as well. Since I've lived in many different countries, I've had to find ways to overcome cultural differences. For example, the tendency for individuals to be tardy to any encounter in Latin America is pretty normal but drove (and still drives) me up the wall. I always arrive five minutes early. I calculate extra time for transport in the case of an emergency. Latin Americans not so much, typically.

Once I spoke with someone who said, "You can either learn to accept their ways or be unhappy forever."

So instead of continuing to be frustrated, I created a list in my phone of topics I wanted to research when I was bored or waiting. Some examples include: circular farming, overcoming cultural disparities, organizations to donate to in Latin America, Socratic seminars, cross-border legal agreements, bed frames on Amazon, water purification methods, cost of sunflower butter in Mexico, etc. Random, but helpful. By having this list of non-essential but interesting topics, I calmed myself down when waiting half an hour for my friend to show up. The time I waited wasn't wasted time, but rather a useful block. I was now more knowledgeable about more concepts or informed myself on something I wanted to know.

Want to know about the Chinese digital Yuan? I got you.

This method also made me realize that others are not late because they hate me. Because yes, that is the first thought that goes through my mind. Rather, they literally just were doing other things and culturally have not placed as much importance on punctuality.

Good thing I have bipolar. I had the foresight to know therapy would help me in some way, and it did. I gained a more flexible, creative mentality to getting over emotional difficulties.

And as a brief aside, which I will expand on more later, for anyone reading this who has had contact with someone with depression or something similar, the only thing I wished during my depressive episodes was for someone to reach out to me and say hi and that they cared. Now, I tell myself that I am strong and can overcome anything. If you can do what you can though, I would say reach out and be thankful for his or her existence.

Later on, per recommendation from the same therapist, I decided to attend some group therapy sessions in addition to my weekly private sessions.

Group therapy makes you feel like you are not alone. Typically, groups are focused on one topic that all the participants have in common. There is a therapist, or two in my case, who leads the session with open-ended questions and activities.

The therapist will ask a question to the group. Either each person will answer one by one in order, or there will be silence until one person decides that they want to go first. Others will chime in one by one after that.

My session had a max capacity of six people, and it was the same six people every week for 12 weeks in a row. Missing was only accepted for legit reasons because each member needed to participate to help the whole group dynamic.

With those people, I could cry and laugh and just be me because they understood. And then hearing their stories and how they decided to overcome them gave me more ideas for getting over my own roadblocks.

Each person in my group was at a different stage in their life and process, which allowed us all to benefit from the others. The individuals further ahead in their process that were looking back were able to be more introspective of how far they had come. Those who were newer to therapy, like me, were able to learn techniques from the more seasoned members.

In addition to therapy, I have also grown to LOVE meditating. Like most people, I didn't get into meditating from one day to the next. It was a gradual integration into my life.

On top of work and school, in college, I was also part of the

"Wellness Advocates," which was a group of chosen individuals on campus who led different workshops on one of three different topics: Mindful Health, Mindful Meditation, and Mindful Sex.

I was an advocate for Mindful Sex, which meant that my workshops dealt with how to ensure that you and your partner(s) are all consensually agreeing to have sex at that moment. I also divided situations into categories of when a person cannot give consent and tactics for making consent sexy. I loved giving those workshops.

However, during the training period and before we were assigned to the specific workshop we would be leading, all the members went through the same training for all workshops. The training, if not obvious already, focused on being mindful in all aspects of your life. Mindfulness was, and to some extent still is, all the rage. Everything needed/needs to be mindful.

During those four full days of training, I was introduced to meditation. I loved it.

After sitting, breathing, and being mindful, I got such a huge boost of natural energy. I had never felt anything like it before. I wanted it to happen again and again.

I had so much mental clarity. For the entire rest of the day, I could focus clearly and handle the regular stress of college life. I couldn't believe it.

However, after those training days, I rarely meditated again. I didn't even try.

I don't think I'm alone in thinking that I just "don't have time to meditate." I came across a Zen saying recently. It states, "You should sit in meditation for 20 minutes a day. Unless you're too busy, then you should sit for an hour."

It makes total sense. Really think about it. Honestly! You and everyone else has at least 20 minutes every day to spare. If you don't think so, you can wake up 20 minutes early, and there you go. Or meditate to fall asleep.

Same thing with eating healthy. No one just "has time" to

religiously meal prep, contemplate each fruit and veggie to make sure it's organic enough to buy, and read all the macro- and micronutrients on the label of every packaged good you buy before getting to the checkout line. No one just has that time. They *make* the time. How dedicated are you to the result?

Same thing with me and my approach to meditation.

I knew I loved meditation, but never did anything about it. Why was I not engaging in an activity I loved? I have no idea.

During the pandemic, USC offered a few online courses to alumni. One was a meditation course. As soon as I saw it, I signed up.

Meditating with a virtual group honestly wasn't that different from meditating with an in-person group. Either way, I still closed my eyes and listened to what the teacher or meditation guide was saying. Whether a visualization or being conscious of breath, I always came out of the class feeling amazing.

Then I started attending yoga classes at a local yoga studio chain, "Core Power Yoga," in Hillcrest in San Diego.

Each yoga session ended in a meditation. Lots of people interpret yoga and meditation as the same thing. Although both are very introspective, they are practiced separately. The first class I went to, I came. Literally! Sexually. Orgasmed. I'm still not sure how Megan, the yoga instructor, managed to do it. We downward dogged and pigeon-folded and tree posed, and when we hit savasana (also known as corpse pose, it's basically just laying down on your back), our final meditation began. She guided us through bliss and light and then…and then…that slight jitter on my inner right thigh that got increasingly stronger. I got a head rush. My eyes probably rolled back in my head, but they were closed, so I'm not sure. I felt myself getting slightly moist between my legs.

I couldn't believe it. Without even touching myself, I came! That's how powerful the mind is. And on another note, how unnecessary a physical sexual partner is—sorry not sorry, guys.

Since that episode, I have successfully meditated myself into an orgasm only one other time. Still completely shocked.

It took me a while to get strong enough to meditate daily myself. My mind would wander. In my mindfulness classes, I was taught not to judge the wandering of the mind, but I could not concentrate at all and got anxious.

That's when I found guided meditations on YouTube and Spotify. I've since found there are great ones on Netflix as well.

I was able to try a broader range of meditations that way. Body positivity, self-love, future planning, culture shock, and…how to not be annoyed by annoying people in public. Yes, there is a guided meditation for that. (I have, however, found much more success just tapping someone on the shoulder and asking them to please use headphones or earbuds for their blast, click, sputter and shoot video games in a public bus.)

After about a year of guided meditation, I ventured out to solo meditation. I started with just two minutes. Breathe. In, out, in, out. Breathe. Relax.

DING! That was the timer. Wasn't so hard.

Then I increased it to five minutes. I'm now at 10. I close my eyes and meditate for 10 minutes every morning after my workout. It keeps me calm and my emotions in check for that day. Sometimes I meditate before bed as well. I'll also meditate in the middle of the day sometimes if I'm stressed or feel my emotions getting slightly pulled to one extreme. I give myself the space to be mindful and cognizant of where I am emotionally in that moment and where I want to be.

My symptoms of bipolar are definitely more in check because of meditation.

If I hadn't meditated in the morning, by the early afternoon, I can already feel that something is off; something peculiar happening in the equilibrium of my emotions.

Thanks, bipolar, for having given me the curiosity to join

random classes that, in the end, made the bipolar easier to handle!

I've also learned to completely and obsessively surround myself with positivity and positive people. I have *extremely* low tolerance for complainers. A few complaints are fine, sure. I need to get things off my chest sometimes as well. But continuous complaining about situations that you can change surpasses my level of patience.

No one else is going to motivate you more than yourself. As much as a partner, best friend, or mentor can cheer you on, you are the only one who can really do the work. Want to lose weight? Your coach can't work out for you. Write a book? Either sit down and write, or work to get the money to pay a ghostwriter. Either way, you still have to work.

Same thing with emotions. I am the only person who can fully ensure that I am happy.

I do that by surrounding myself with people who are positive influences. My dad, for example, is great. Karla, a close friend of mine in Mexico, is also a great example.

When other people are busy or I do not feel like going out, then I rely on social media. Yes, social media makes me feel better. I consciously choose to not follow accounts that make me feel bad. I follow comedians, dancing accounts, friends, body positive accounts, pets accounts, etc.

The Kardashians? Sorry, I don't have a perfect enough body.

This comes from a very privileged point of view, I understand. For example, I have never had a close family member die, so I definitely do not understand what that pain feels like. Also, I've never had body dysmorphia nor an eating disorder, so I can't comprehend, on a personal level, the pain of body comparison. However, I have my own views of the world that make ultra-positive content necessary.

I follow people like Gary V, Grant Cardone, Tony Robbins, Ed Mylett, and more who talk about the mindset that you should have in order to live a successful life.

From afar, Gary V teaches me to be grateful. Grant Cardone teaches me to dream big. Tony Robbins how to motivate myself, and Ed Mylett to never give up.

I also enjoy female, feminist comedians and memoirists such as Whitney Cummings, Ali Wong, Iliza Schlessinger, Glennon Doyle, and Kristina Kuzmič, who show me that it's okay to mess up and being a woman is awesome.

THOSE are the influences that I need on social media.

I also follow a slew of healthy eating pages for inspiration for new recipes. I follow travel pages for ideas and a handful of meme pages because, to be completely honest, memes are funny, make me laugh, and I like a good chuckle.

When I come across someone who is consistently negative in my life, I just stop planning outings with him or her. It's not necessary to make up a whole show about why I don't want to be close. They are not bad people, just not the influences I require to keep my own emotions in check.

If I am the average of my five closest friends, the saying says, well, hell, I'm going to make sure that those are the best influences I can find.

* * *

Therapy in Latin America is slightly different than therapy in the States. Per personal experience, it's better. But every individual can come to their own conclusion after trying.

After a few years without therapy, the pandemic hit. I had planned to move to Brazil from Peru to study my Masters' degree in language education. I got a full scholarship! But due to the pandemic, the Brazilian university, Universidade Federal do Espírito Santo, closed its door to foreigners, Peru fully closed its borders to international travel, and I, having gone to the States to get my student visa at the Brazilian embassy in LA, was now stuck at my parent's house in San Diego. Not exactly the American dream nor teenage dream nor a twenty-three-year old's dream.

I wasn't making enough money from my Latin America-based outsourcing job to survive in the US by myself.

I had lost all sense of independence. I was spiraling. The time had come to look for therapy again.

Finding a therapist in the US is a thousand times harder than in Latin America. I have no idea why. There's probably someone who can explain it. I know the US has a thousand necessary certifications for a therapist to practice legally and weak health insurance or private funding makes sessions extremely expensive. And labor laws about how many hours they work or how many patients they can have.

In Latin America, there is more flexibility. I wasn't looking for a psychiatrist or someone who could prescribe me medication. For that, yes, clearly, I want my doctor to have every certification available. I just wanted someone who would just listen.

When I figured out that there was more availability and accessibility to therapists in Latin America, my search began. Luckily, I speak fluent Spanish. As mentioned, my dad is Peruvian. He spoke Spanish to me my entire life. Plus, growing up in San Diego, speaking Spanish is a real plus since it's right on the border with Tijuana.

I had to start over with "dating" new therapists. I had a few weird sessions, but nothing that made me feel bad.

One Ecuadorian therapist had me burn paper in my room as a ritual to release the bad energy. (Since this was during the pandemic, all the sessions were remote.) It felt oddly comforting, although it wasn't quite hitting what I wanted to discuss. With her, I also had to draw a bunch of pictures in a notebook. It was successful to get my mind off my daily tasks, but again, it didn't get to the point of why I was in therapy.

I ended up having my last sessions with a therapist in the US. We had three sessions total, but I couldn't fork up the $200 per session anymore. In Latin America, I pay between $30-$60 per hour.

Then I found Lorena. Lorena reminded me a lot of my first therapist.

Lorena let me speak my thoughts without interrupting. She has quite a multi-cultural background as well, which made me feel that she understood me from the core better than mono-cultural therapists (either Latin or American) because there was the added factor of cultural integration no matter where I lived. She asked questions that led me into deeper explanations of my feelings.

At the end of each session with Lorena, we either do a meditation, a visualization, or a stretch. For me, that's an added bonus that I love.

Therapy is great. It just takes a while to find the right therapist.

A therapist helps to constantly refine my superpower to use it the way that I should. Similar to why children go to school to learn to use their brains for completing certain tasks, you learn to use the brain you were given. Why do you hire a workout coach or join a group class at the gym? To learn how to use your body, the machines, and the weights correctly. Therapy helps you learn to use your emotions correctly.

There isn't any other place where you are allowed to work on your brain and the emotions it emotes. And society judges therapy negatively for no logical reason.

Everyone I know who goes to therapy comes out stronger. And is actually easier to interact with because, after having had time to work on themselves, they now have the time to work on others.

Therapy sharpened my superpower. Therapy made my bipolarity a strength, my superpower.

Similar to therapy is life coaching. I have had multiple intro conversations with life and business coaches to really understand the difference.

In summary, a therapist helps you get through your past problems. You work through childhood traumas (or adult ones, like my case) and through tools that you can use to be a better person in the present.

Coaching is the next step. At first, if you want, you can overlap your coaching and therapy as you make the transition. Coaching looks towards the future and helps you develop a plan for your next steps. You learn what base you need in order to achieve your goal in a specified amount of time, typically coaches start a plan for anywhere from three to six months but can adjust to what you are planning to do and what you want to accomplish.

My first coach was a sales coach. She opened my eyes to the wonders of coaching. I find it socially common for people not to stay as true to themselves as they should. It's seen as selfish in society to be focusing only on yourself. With a coach, someone else is making you reliant. You have weekly tasks or homework to complete to achieve your goal.

Yes, you are working on yourself, but someone else is outlining the steps you need to take in order to get there.

The sales coaching program was specifically designed for 12 consecutive weeks with specific material that needed to be watched each week coupled with weekly meetings and monthly one-on-one strategy sessions. I loved it. I had someone to be accountable towards.

In my case, *paying* helped. Did I want to fork up five grand for the course? Absolutely not. However, because I paid, I was more incentivized to actually show up and do the work.

And I increased my sales because of it! I became way better than I could have ever imagined.

A few months later, I interviewed for a new job at a much larger corporation in essentially the same industry. My previous client contracts that I managed ranged from $24,000-30,000 yearly (per contract). This new company averaged clients paying a few million dollars for a three-year set contract with possibility to expand and work with huge international corporations like Revlon, the makeup company.

It was a huge opportunity, and the base and commission structure were much more than I was earning elsewhere.

However, after interviews with four different individuals in the company, I wasn't 100 percent convinced that this was the professional environment for me.

In my back pocket, I had a few life and motivational coaches I knew I could reach out to.

I emailed one and asked for what I called an "emergency meeting." (I know, I'm dramatic.) Think of it as those "on call" therapists who help you when you're in the middle of a panic or anxiety attack.

Clearly I was not in an attack, but I had a limited time to make a decision on my next step and needed to make sure I was making it for the right reasons, morally and professionally.

No one in the company was bad, per say. But I didn't have that automatic "click" with them.

Should I grow and learn to work with individuals with different personalities? Afterall, this was a workplace and not a playground. Or should I continue looking elsewhere where I can find a "work best friend"?

Keep in mind that, in other companies, I always felt the freedom to also talk about topics not related to work, which is 100 percent necessary in a workplace. Being able to relax is important.

The coach responded to my email almost immediately, and we set up a call for the following morning. We chatted.

I spent the first 20 minutes just describing my situation to give a little background on why I was frustrated.

I started by quoting a line from her book that directly related to how I was feeling:

I am in a situation where I feel stuck. Fear of the future is developing into anxiety. And my anxiety is turning me into a victim of anger, resentment, frustration, hopelessness and depression. (*Grow a Pair of Antlers*, Kathleen Ries-Jubenville)

Going into the call, I had assumed I would cry, but somehow, I kept it together there and only fell apart later on in public in a Victoria's Secret while shopping for lingerie. That was a fun experience. Not that I cared much what other people were thinking, but they probably thought something along the lines of "that girl just got dumped" or "she probably feels fat looking at all the Victoria's Secret model pictures." In reality, I just felt lost in general.

The actual call with the coach gave me lots of clarity in making a decision. We went through the pros and cons of each direction that I could take. We also made a list of my non-negotiables. Having them written down makes it easier to quickly disqualify opportunities that don't fully meet my needs, emotionally or otherwise. The lists weren't daunting. Maximum four bullet points for each list. This condensed all my thoughts down to just the bare essentials, so I could compare options.

Different from a therapist, we didn't look at the reasons I felt the way I felt and find yet more reasons to cope with those emotions.

Together, we just started with "this is how I feel right now, and this is what I'm looking for in six months."

Then, based on what is there in the moment, we built for the future.

I took notes myself during the meeting. I would consider it a business meeting for myself and my professional life. There was strategy, data input and analysis, and an expected result. The result would first be revealed in a few months if the strategy was followed correctly.

Most people I've chatted with either don't know about coaching or undervalue it. People who don't know about it can inform themselves through books like the one you are reading or by reaching out to other coaches online. Google: life coaches, emotional coaches, freedom coaches, financial coaches, business coaches, etc.

People who undervalue coaching typically don't like that

coaches are not obligated to have any sort of certification. It isn't like being a psychologist or therapist who needs to go through a series of tests and certifications to legally practice on patients. There are coaching certification programs online and in-person. They are not *mandatory* though. A coach can read a few books and speak from life experience and, boom, call themselves a coach. If that's all they did, clearly they wouldn't be getting much business nor much success with clients, but if they want the title, boom, they have it.

Personally, if the individual has been in the field for years, is making a living off what they are doing, and has shown that they constantly re-educated themselves with new material being published, I'm alright if my coach is not a Doctor of Psychology.

Coaches help harness my superpower for the future, just like therapists do for the present.

CHAPTER 4

Taking Risks

I've spoken a lot about the depressive episodes.

Now I want to touch on the positive parts of bipolar.

With bipolar, there are manic episodes. Those. Are. Great! Excellent, if I do say so myself. I am all-mighty, enchanting, sexy, smart, funny, outgoing, enjoyable company, and more!

The best part is the ideas. The ideas flow like water downhill on a slippery slope with zero friction. They just keep coming. Good ideas, at that. I start planning and detailing exactly how I will get what I want.

Here are some examples of projects I pursued initially while in a manic episode:

- **Getting accepted with a full scholarship to study my master's in Brazil.**

    I started and finished the entire application in one weekend. I didn't end up going because of COVID-related reasons.

    At the time of writing the application, I had already taught myself Portuguese, initially just for fun, and I had investigated a lot about Brazilian culture. I even spent time in the Portuguese language library in the Brazilian embassy in Lima, Peru, went to zouk dancing classes, a typical partner dance in Brazil, and listened to lots of Brazilian funk on Spotify, similar in popularity to reggaeton in Hispano-America.

I had read that Brazilian universities offered great packages for foreigners, and I had wanted to get my master's.

I took the Brazilian Portuguese fluency exam, CELPE-Bras but hadn't gotten the results yet.

One weekend, I hit the ground running and decided that I had all the pieces I would need: fluency exam results pending, potential recommenders (who hadn't actually written letters yet), and a bachelor's degree.

What was missing? A 4,000-word essay on a thesis project I would pursue, a 2,000-word motivation letter about why I wanted to study in Brazil, two recommendation letters, and all my legal documentation, like birth certificate, passport scans, etc. And what was written by me, was to be written in Portuguese.

I started and finished everything that weekend. Including writing both recommendation letters myself and having my boss and an ex-coworker-turned-CEO sign off on them. Turns out this is more common than you'd think. Lots of students write their own letters of rec and have their recommender just review, tweak, and sign them.

Clearly my writing skills during my manic episode were superb because I got accepted!

- ***Quit my office job (because who needs one of those?) and decided to go fully remote without any remote experience.***
Keep in mind, this was a year and a half before COVID hit, so a 22-year-old going remote was not normal.

My dad had been working remotely since I was about six, so I knew it was possible.

I must have put some good mojo out into the universe because I got a fully remote job three weeks after quitting.

Additionally, the pay was double what I was making, AND the new company was going to pay for me to go to Costa Rica for two months for training. Count me in!

- ***Getting funded to study in Italy.***

I graduated with my undergraduate degree in Rome, Italy.

I had already taken three years of Italian in college just to fill up spaces in my schedule. One day, I decided to apply to a program and separate scholarship to study in Italy. My university offered students the ability to take "mini semesters" abroad, all I needed was the funding for it. I got both the funding and acceptance to the course! Buongiorno, Italia!

- ***Being a finalist to study in Azerbaijan.***

If you haven't realized already, languages are central to my identity. I applied to an intensive program that would send me to Baku, the capital of Azerbaijan.

Similar to my application to study in Brazil, I also wrote the entire application in one weekend to go to Azerbaijan to study the language and culture.

I detailed how an intense, immersive program learning Azerbaijani would allow me a wider cultural breadth to represent the US abroad and back home by having an inclusive and understanding manner, which could help to solve unnecessary conflict down the line.

I was a semi-finalist, set to be a replacement in the case that one of the selected winners couldn't go. Apparently, they all could because I did not end up in Azerbaijan.

I would consider that more than a semi-finalist, though. A replacement finalist. Not too bad!

Of all the above-mentioned activities though, one of the biggest risks I took was moving to Peru after college.

Yes, I had been to Peru plenty of times before. But it was always just to wallow away at the clubs, take trips to Cuzco and Iquitos, or enjoy a pisco sour at Restaurante-Bar "Haiti" overlooking the Óvalo de Miraflores in Parque Kennedy.

Before moving to Peru, I had studied at the University of Southern California. A world renowned, accredited, and established university. It also lies at the top of the list for most expensive universities in the world with a starting price tag of $63,000 per year for on-campus students when I was a freshman. (The price has increased 5 percent every year since my graduation.)

Neither my parents nor I had the money to pay the price upfront. I took out a student loan.

Freshman year, I started working one job, and as the years progressed, I took on more roles in addition to the first. By my third year, I was working three jobs and taking 20 credits, while the normal was 16 credits per semester.

I did it to graduate one year early, save money, and start paying off my loans sooner.

By the time graduation came around, I had $53,273 in student debt and a monthly minimum payment of $535.

Moving to Peru did not guarantee a job that would allow me to make stable monthly payments toward the loan, pay my rent, buy food, *and* save and/or invest.

I didn't care.

Everyone seemed to, except my parents. My parents were very supportive, although their faces were a bit wary when I said I had landed a job that paid only $1,000 per month.

For perspective, minimum wage in that year in the United States was just over $2,000 and with my monthly loan payments just above $500, it meant I would only have $500 to live.

As my foreign-born therapist had yelled at me years earlier,

I would have no room for growth, savings, or further education in Peru.

I moved anyway. And my parents ended up supporting part of my monthly payments.

The day of the move was more emotional than I had anticipated, although I hid it at the moment. All three of my parents were there, mom, dad, and stepdad. We met up at LAX. I had driven up from San Diego with my mom and stepdad that morning while my dad drove from Las Vegas to see me part.

I checked in my luggage and got my boarding pass. As expected, both my checked suitcases were significantly overweight, and I had to pay $100 extra just to get them on the plane. I wasn't surprised.

I went back to my parents for some last words. I thanked them for everything and got parting gifts from each.

We walked together from the check-in area at the front of the Tom Bradley Terminal to the back escalators that led up to the security check.

My parents weren't allowed on the second floor without a boarding pass, so we said our final goodbyes there. I wouldn't be back in the States for almost a year.

Standing in the security line on the second floor, I could see the busy motions of everything that was happening below. The line was moving slowly, so I had time to spot my parents.

Although I couldn't hear what they were saying from 500 feet away, I could tell they were having friendly chit chat.

Both my mom and dad had shed a few tears at the goodbye. I hadn't. But up on the second floor, hidden from their view because of the distance, I cried.

I was so thankful that everyone got along, especially given my parents got divorced, and typically divorced parents don't have friendly chit chat with the new husband/wife of their ex-partner.

They were also all so supportive of me moving, even though

I wouldn't be making much money.

I cried because I was nervous. In two days' time, I would already be starting my first day at my first ever full-time job out of college.

I had bought new work clothes: two new dress shirts with matching dress pants and pumps for the office. I had never owned anything like it.

I had asked my grandma if I could stay with her upon my arrival in Peru until I found a place of my own. She accepted. But that meant that upon arrival I really had nowhere of my own to stay. I had to look for that, too.

I was nervous for the next few days and everything I had to set up.

I needed to set up my health insurance, a phone plan, and figure out how to get to the office building I would work at.

Looking out over the crowd of people checking in and saying goodbye to their loved ones, I got increasingly more nervous. What was I doing? I was 21 and moving to a different continent!

Peru was technically already home to me. I had family and most of my friends there. I knew I had a support system if necessary. But honestly, what was I doing?!

Looking back now, it was the best decision I could've made. I don't regret it at all.

Let's take a step back. How did I end up landing a job in Peru before getting there anyway?

My dad taught me that not having a job means that my only job is to find a job. That's right. Eight hours EVERY. DAY. Four hours of applications in the morning. Lunch break. And four hours of applications in the afternoon. No excuses!

I applied to every job on LinkedIn that required someone that spoke English. Although I speak fluent Spanish, I figured I would have a better shot at a job that needed a fluent English speaker and could interact with international markets or clients. I was right.

I got hired as a salesperson for a SaaS company based in Peru but with predominantly US clients.

Because of my native English skills, the CEO needed me. This gave me a strong approximation to leadership and management, something that would have never happened so quickly for your average 21-year-old recent college graduate.

This job also provided an intensive sales course where I learned the ins and outs of sales through Grant Cardone.

Because of this proximity, I was an ideal candidate for my following job, a Costa Rican-based software development outsourcing company. I also needed to understand sales and work in the US market. There I earned twice as much as the first company!

Low and behold, the job I switched to during the pandemic, an Australian-based outsourcing company, was looking for a sales professional in the US market. And, whoopdy-do, paid also twice as much as the last.

Finally, I'd be getting paid a sustainable US salary, *and* I was put in charge of running a team of three. Would I have otherwise had that opportunity as a 23-year-old had I not moved to Peru? I think not.

I had the experience working directly with upper management, proximity to clients, and leading teams, which put me above pretty much an average person.

Add on that I got and continue to have experiences in other countries, which the majority of Americans envy greatly.

Moving to Peru was great, and I don't regret it or any other thing that I started on a manic episode.

Whereas I've shared the successes, there have, of course, been projects I started that never went anywhere.

Here are some things that got started during a manic episode and never got traction:

- One time, I tried to start drop shipping a company for

kitchen supplies. I got it legally registered, got a website, and got inventory, only to drop out one month later.
- I started a company through AmWay more or less at the same time. Didn't go anywhere either. I sold detergent to my mom and gave out free mascara to my friends.
- I studied for the GRE for two months with the plan to go to Harvard Grad school. I had convinced myself that Harvard was my destiny. Still not sure why. Never took the exam and never went to Harvard.
- I tried to start a podcast. Quit after episode two. They are probably still out there somewhere in ether space. But I can't remember what platform I used to publish them, so I can't find them. I also can't remember the name of the podcast. If you find them, please free free to contact me and share them.
- A girl I had met once on tinder asked if I wanted to visit her in Chile. I booked my flight two days later to visit her at the end of the month. She wasn't there when I arrived. Chile was fun though, so not a total loss.
- I wanted to be a work coach by holding workshops for people in Lima, Peru, that focused on how to make a great resume and optimize your LinkedIn profile. I made a PowerPoint and even talked it through with the head recruiter from the company I was at. He helped give the idea more form and value. Then I just never did anything after that.
- Tried to buy a house in Peru. Failed after I couldn't find an international mortgage. That being said, I'm currently trying to buy an apartment in Mexico. I already have an approval on the mortgage. One step closer! Not a total flop.

In my professional career, working remote and managing my own schedule helps SO much. I can pump out more work when I am energized and lean back a little more when I am not on much of a high. I use this to my advantage. Typically on manic episodes, I plan out the steps that I need to take every day to reach X goal. By the time I'm back to being normal or even low-energy, I rely on the creativity that I took advantage of during the manic episode and just blindly follow the "instructions" I gave myself.

For example, starting an acting career is difficult and requires consistent applying to castings. The beginning of each casting video requires you share your personal information (height, weight, measurements, etc.), and then you do a small scene based on what the casting asks for.

In order to quicken the process, I created a drag-and-drop template for all my castings. I recorded myself doing the intro with all possible information a casting director would want and saved it separately. Then, I obligated myself to do at least one casting per week, if not more if I had the time and energy. Creating the videos was quick. All I had to do was a 30-second acting and then plop it into my template. I sent out a bunch. Three weeks after I started with this method, I was booked and on-set filming my first commercial for a new credit card company!

I do the same thing for my day job in sales. Sales is a bipolar role in and of itself, let's be honest. There are good months and bad months. It's a rollercoaster. What I can control is how many people I reach out to on a daily basis. On the downside, I'm not motivated to prospect every day. On the upside, when I prospect, I prospect HARD. And I mean reach out to 300 people in one day for three days straight. On this note, it definitely helps to have a virtual assistant that does prospecting on a more stable basis. Keeps leads coming in fluidly, instead of periods with a lot and then nothing.

Overall, instead of saying "I can't do it because I'm bipolar," I say, "I can't do it your way, but I can do it my way."

Moving to Peru wasn't the only big risk that I have taken.

Quitting is hard for me and something that I need to get more used to practicing.

Since high school, I've had the tendency to take on multiple projects at once. I loved them, and I love staying busy.

Whereas my thoughts are a bit scattered by nature and my bedroom floor is usually not visible thanks to the clothes laying around, I am extremely organized in my work and school life.

I follow my calendar to a "T" and keep different folders and notebooks of organized information I need for each class or personal life subject. In school, my folders were organized in order of the classes that I attended each week. Assignments were written down in my agenda and were completed daily. I HATE unfinished checklists. Checklists work great for me. Writer's workshop, statistics, intro chemistry, biology, syntax and semantics, morphology, second language acquisition, etc. Each class had a folder.

For work, I'm the same. My email has folders, sub folders, and sub-subfolders of the information that I need to keep. My folder structure looks something like the following:

- **Internal**
    - Correspondences with CEO
    - Correspondences with Direct Boss
    - Finance
        - Need to pay
        - Getting paid
- Recruitment
    - Internal roles
    - External roles
- Save for later
- Marketing
    - Correspondences with marketing team
    - Updates from each member

- **External**
    - Sales
        - Clients
        - Prospects
        - Leads
    - Contractors
    - Services Providers

I integrated my personal and work calendars so that I can see everything I need to do in one view.

I use Google Calendar, so I can color code my activities. Here's an example of how I code:
- Yellow= client meetings
- Blue= internal meeting
- Gray= break/eat
- Red= class/workshop/education
- Green= networking event
- Purple= personal time and other personal events

(such as therapy sessions or working out)

I also typically log when I need to travel from one area to another. Ten minutes walking to a café to work? Logged. Need to drive to an in-person client meeting? Logged. Need to travel to the airport? Logged.

Timewise, handling lots of activities is not necessarily my problem. I try my best to analyze how an activity will fit into my schedule before taking it on. Although, I rarely say no to something that I know will give me joy and advance either my career or social standing (or happiness, I guess).

During my summer breaks in high school, I took on many activities. The summer before senior year, I volunteered for 40 hours per week at a child day care facility. I was cheer captain and had to run all the fundraising events for the competitions that we needed to pay for throughout the year. I ended up running the largest fundraiser that the cheer team had run till up until then, bringing in four times more profit than any other event, and I was pre-studying for all of my classes I would take senior year. I was also studying for the SAT and ACT and prepping my college applications.

In college, as previously mentioned, I worked three jobs, volunteered at the wellness center, and took 20 credits per semester.

After college, in a way, work seemed easier. It was just one activity. Everything else I did didn't seem as obligatory, but either way, I started taking on bigger projects.

As a side note, I extremely dislike when people cancel plans on me. The planned activity was most likely in the calendar, color-coded, and meditated on. I need to prepare for social interactions. I have since come up with a strategy for dealing with this, which I previously discussed.

With such high organization, it takes a lot for me to quit something. If it's already on my mind and scheduled, I don't want to take it off.

I have no idea where this mindset came from. My mom is very lax. She never forced me to be this harsh with my academics or profession. She also said it was okay if I got a B in a class instead of an A, which was *not* okay with me.

All that being said, I start a lot of projects that are not finished, but that doesn't mean I feel good when they end. I feel horrible.

I am just starting to realize the benefit of quitting though.

I can't do everything, and I need to accept that.

In Peru, I was working an office-based job. I hated going into the office every day. Or maybe it wasn't the actual office because having coworkers is fun. You always have someone to gossip with.

I had seen my dad work remotely for 15-plus years at that point and wanted that, too. I felt the oncoming of a traveler's heart.

Since I was working in Peru and attending to the US market and US clients, there shouldn't have been a problem with remote work. Everyone I needed to talk to was not physically close anyway.

My boss did not like that. He rejected my request.

That's when I took a leap. I turned in a three-week notice; plenty of time for them to adjust. I had no other job on the line.

Through LinkedIn, however, I ended up getting in contact with the CEO of another company who liked my profile. I interviewed with them one day after my shift ended at my office job.

The head recruiter called me a few days later and offered me the position, working remotely.

Quitting was great! It gave me the space to accept something amazing in the place of something that was draining me.

A similar thing happened a few years later. This time, however, within the same employment.

I came on as a salesperson; however, I was also leading up the internal digital marketing team. Albeit a small team, there was no previous leader. I had experience with some digital marketing tasks from my previous employment, so the CEO and direct manager of the current company saw it fit that I oversee what each member in the DM team was doing.

I was good at asking questions. I knew which projects needed to be completed, and I knew all the DM terminology. I was technically on the DM team in my previous employment and had to run campaigns for lead generation. I could explain PPC campaigns, SEO, and A/B tests. Looking at it from his point of view, I understand why it seemed like I knew what I was doing.

However, knowing what the terms are and being able to manage a team is very different.

I am in favor of individual excellence and a hero in every role, terms I learned from reading *Atomic Habits* by James Clear.

Individual excellence means that you don't have to be promoted into a managerial role, but rather be compensated in your current role if that is where you are happy and what you're good at. For those who want to be managers, that is completely fine as well, but it shouldn't be seen as the only form of professional growth.

The skills needed to complete a task and manage a team are different, but that doesn't mean that one role is more important than the other.

Businesses tend to promote into managerial roles, thinking that this type of lateral movement is the natural next step when it's actually not.

A person should be promoted to where he or she works best. And those who are great at the role they are currently in should get compensated by how they are most motivated. Want a salary increase? How about the same salary but 25 percent more vacation days per year? Maybe you actually do want to be a manager? All are totally valid appraisals to a good employee.

There are a lot of great managers, but not everyone is meant to be in that role. I am one of those people.

Managing the DM team was great. But I have proven to not have as strong an execution in that position as I have in a sales role. Admitting that I couldn't be a manager was emotionally draining in itself.

One benefit of sales, I believe, over other roles is the uncapped earning potential and the direct correlation between your input and earnings.

The more time and effort you spend on targeted prospecting, the more qualified prospects you generated, the more closed deals you have, and the higher commissions you earn.

If I want a vacation? Yes, I totally earned it. But no lead generation during that time. So...well, you get the point.

I had led the digital marketing team for almost a full year by December 2021.

In the first week of January 2022, I picked up the previously mentioned book, *Atomic Habits*, and it changed my path.

I finally realized that although a managerial title on my LinkedIn profile looked cool, executing it wasn't allowing me to yield the best outcome for either myself or the business.

I voluntarily asked my direct supervisor if I could step away from managing and focus 100 percent on sales. To not leave gaps, I put in a strong recommendation for a member of the DM team who had previously voiced wanting to grow into a leadership position and who had many more years working in digital marketing than I had.

My boss agreed. It made sense.

Two months later, I had increased my monthly sales three times in comparison to my monthly average from the year prior.

I could finally focus on what I was really good at, although I didn't realize how good I could be at it till I allowed myself the space and focus to grow in it.

Again, quitting allowed me the time and mental space to focus on an activity that would give me an overall better yield on happiness, clients, and income than before.

Wow!! I guess quitting isn't that bad after all.

Quitting and setting limits has now become extremely important to me. I learned this through personal practice in social situations, as well.

By being in a different culture, I learned more about how to talk to people about being bipolar, or not talk about it at all.

Being bipolar isn't exactly a topic that you share on a first date or when you first meet someone in class.

From my experience, anyone diagnosed with a mental disorder judges others for quite some time before deciding to share.

There are typically two roads people can choose when opening up.

I'll use being bipolar here as the example, but it can be any diagnosis:

1. "I was *diagnosed* with bipolar disorder. This is just a diagnosis but does not represent me. I still have the freedom to create my personality as I feel fit."

2. "I *am* bipolar. There is nothing I can do about it. I will figure out my own way to solve problems using bipolarity. It may be different than yours but that's okay."

The first option separates the individual from being bipolar. The second option embraces being bipolar.

I think both can be effective at empowering any person with bipolar, depending on his or her personal life situations.

Personally, I have found more success following the second option. I am bipolar. I will solve my problems one way or another. I probably will not do it your way, but somehow, I'll do it.

* * *

I also learned to measure people heavily until I was alright with
sharing that I am bipolar. While getting to know someone, I will typically ask them questions like these:
- What books do you read?
- Do you have anyone with a mental illness in your family?

I won't tell them out of the blue. I will, of course, weave the topic into conversation.

I'll also bring up news articles about the topic and ask what they think.

Based on their reaction, I can decide if I will later share. Sometimes I never do.

Clearly I'm becoming more and more confident about the topic because I'm writing this book about it. Unfortunately, it's a lot more intimidating to share the information with someone when you haven't had the chance to prove you can be successful first.

If I told someone preemptively, they would automatically

judge me and say that I will never be able to finish a project or get a good job.

Sure, I start things that don't get finished. But the things I finish are great. And when have you ever had a huge influx of amazing ideas? Do you ever feel on top of the world?

Now that I've proven that I can still hold a job for…well, at least a year and a half, show a positive change in the business, create something from nothing, be financially independent, and more, I do have a bit more material to work with when chatting with people about the topic.

Bipolar people can be SO successful!

And that's also proven by many A-listers that have openly spoken about being bipolar. Some examples are: Demi Lovato, Mariah Carey, Taylor Tomlinson, Mel Gibson, Russel Brand, Frank Sinatra, and…Winston Churchill!

Guess that manic high does get you to some great places. You just have to focus it on the right projects.

Being bipolar is NOT synonymous with being dumb, being unsuccessful, being dispassionate, being rude, being aggressive, and more.

Each bipolar person is different, and the symptoms manifest themselves in different ways.

I choose to be grateful for what I have and work with the tools I was given. I get amazing, natural rushes that get me pumped for life and full of ideas for great projects.

I do get depressed, but I was lucky enough to be presented with a box of emotional tools from my therapists and lessons from books that I can use to my advantage to get through the bad times.

I can interact with people around the world, taking into consideration their cultural background and make the best experience out of every situation possible.

Who can judge that negatively?? I feel bad for whoever feels the need to be looking negatively at the life that I have so fruitfully grown for myself.

How boring it would be to not be bipolar! I love my superpower.

CHAPTER 5

Sex and Relationships

Since I was 18, I haven't lived in the same place (either city or apartment within a city) for more than nine months at a time. Once I stayed 11 months in one apartment but not willingly, and I traveled out a lot. I get bored extremely easily.

That goes for relationships as well. Honestly, I'm not unhappy being single. I wouldn't say "no" to a relationship with someone I click well with, but I'm not searching for anyone. People typically don't seem to understand my wackiness. And I fill myself with joy, so who needs another person anyway?

Both my mom and dad are extremely open-minded regarding sex. My mom will make comments on condom commercials:

"Well, practicing baby-making is fun," she would say.

My dad gives me way too many details about his sex life, things that I doubt any daughter typically hears.

Sometimes he's more vulgar than others. But he's shared with no filter.

That being said, both taught me that consensual sex is sexy and safe sex is mandatory. It would not be fun to be with someone who doesn't really want to be with you. That's probably why I have never chased someone who hasn't shown explicit interest in me, at least yet. Also, my mom got me on birth control as soon as I said I wanted to start having sex. And condoms were always available.

Because of my parental influence, I enjoy free, casual, and

frequent sex and am not turned off by people who do the same.

On the dating front, since I started college, I haven't "dated" anyone for more than four months. Usually around month three, I get bored or annoyed with the other person. Either way, most of those people for me have been "open relationships." That doesn't mean I don't get deep feelings for some of them. It always hurts to end something, and if someone treated me unfairly, of course, I'm hurt.

That being said, I know that I've also broken quite a few hearts.

I can't remember if I have ever ended a relationship in person. A quick text is basically my go-to option. I know; I'm a devil.

When I get bored or annoyed, I decide that the negativity is just not meant for me and want to remove it from my life as quickly as possible.

It's definitely something I am working on.

By the time I was 24, my free and casual sex lifestyle had already got me to a total 55 total sexual partners. I have periods of wanting to have a serious relationship and think that sex will get in the way, then do not find anyone I think is worth it and go back to free sex. I never feel bad about it though. I think my main goal should be find a nice balance between some casual sex and also choosing people who are good influences.

I'm not the most innocent person though.

I have had sex with my friend's friends even after they specifically told me not to. Once I was invited on a group date…and then fucked someone else's date. I've had sex with multiple of my ex's friends, never while we were dating. I'm actually quite faithful when I decide to be. I just rarely ever decide to be. I've had sex with people almost 20 years older than me. And I've had sex with people from all over the world: Germany, Peru, Argentina, Nepal, the US, Mexico, Costa Rica, Italy…my list goes on. Black, white, brown, blue, green—honestly, whatever skin color. I had sex with a coworker once (surprisingly, it wasn't awkward come Monday morning).

I have a preference for long hair, on both men and females, but it's not a make it or break it trait, nor is any other physical appearance. I also tend to prefer a little bit more "meaty" people. Too thin or too muscular turns me off. I feel like I'm snuggling with a log and much prefer some fluff.

I once put a brief pause on my sexual scurry. I woke up to the unanticipated text that just said, "Did you already know you had herpes before we had sex?"

What a way to wake up. No "hello." No "good morning." No "hey, there's a topic I need to talk to you about. It's serious. Could you let me know when you're available?" Nope.

I should also mention, it had been four months since I last had sex with the person who texted me, and we only talked a little in between because that friend was busy at work, and I was travelling around.

Still, the message scared the shit out of me, understandably.

I had never once had any symptom of herpes, or any other STI. Being very conscious about my fuckery, I took and still take safety very seriously. I have a birth control implant and use condoms. I've also been vaccinated from everything that I possibly could.

I ended up paying almost $300 while in a foreign country to get a herpes 1 and 2 CPR test. When I walked into the clinic, the doctor asked me a bunch of questions about symptoms, of which I had none and had to explain that it had come to my attention that a previous sexual partner may have tested positive for herpes. I got tested and came back negative.

I paid an extra $250 for an exam that tested for HPV, HIV, gonorrhea, syphilis, and general vagina stuff. I also came back negative for those. I typically get tested once a year anyway, but I went for the extra testing this time around.

Turning a negative, scary moment into a positive one, at least I went and got those check-ups for STIs.

I tried my best to be supportive of my previous sex partner

since clearly he came back positive for herpes. He must have clearly been going through a lot of really rough emotions and was just trying to find out where/who it came from specifically.

Knowing him, I knew he also had sex with a lot of other people, so it was very possible that a few nights after our last soiree, he caught it from someone else. My heart goes out to him.

Maybe he decided to approach the situation that way as a way to ensure that I got tested, while trying to keep himself off the hook for being a possible transmitter. Undoubtedly, he was extremely scared himself.

Either way, I was off put by the way that he approached the topic with me. After sending him the results to all my lab exams to prove that I was negative for everything, we haven't had much contact.

A few months later, he wrote to me again and apologized for the way he approached the topic. I accepted and said I would definitely be emotionally present if he needed anything and have kept my promise the other times that he has reached out.

I do wish him all the best because, above all, I know that he is still a great person at the core. I don't discount the idea that it is statistically possible that I contract an STD. I definitely take stronger measures now than before to ensure that sex is safe.

After this situation, I took a huge chill pill on having sex, just as a way to emotionally recover from the reverberating effects of potentially having contracted an STI.

I actually have multiple close friends with STIs, and speaking with them, I realized, with modern medicine, it really isn't the end of the world.

Some have more serious symptoms than others, of course, but I do have to count my blessings in this situation.

I have health insurance, enough additional money for emergencies, and access to treatments and medicines in the countries where I predominantly reside to ensure that my life would not end because of any STI if it were found in a reasonable timeframe after having been contracted.

Taking precautions while having sex in a non-monogamous fashion is extremely important, and I highly recommend it to everyone, of ALL sexes. Girls, too, can buy condoms. And girls can definitely say NO when there isn't enough protection to their liking.

I've heard male birth control methods are now a thing? Not sure if they are on the market yet, but no doubt in a few years they will be for sure. So everyone involved can ensure that they are doing their part to have a safe, consensual, and enjoyable experience.

Bouncing from one person to another has refined my flirting skills quite a bit.

* * *

Reading both books and articles about human interaction and then putting the theories to the test in real life have granted me quite the positive yield.

I know exactly what type of pictures to post on social media apps so that I am seen as more attractive. Turns out, small quirks or imperfections, not huge ones, can actually make someone more approachable. It does not intimidate other people. I once watched an interview with Kendall and Kylie Jenner. They both admitted to not being flirted with as much as one would think because others seem too intimidated either by their fame or beauty. Granted, that's quite a stretch on where I am, but I hope that gets my point across. I'm perfectly imperfect.

I don't do well with competition in this case, so the easiest way for me to pique someone's interest is to only accept or offer dates that are one on one.

I rarely talk about myself and my accomplishments with new

people I meet because I want to make sure that they talk as much about themselves as possible.

Humans are naturally selfish people and like to talk about themselves. They feel that they have stronger connections with people and are more impressed with the other person when they only talk about themselves. Ironic. Oh, humans!

Since I grew up tricultural, have traveled a lot, and am pretty well read, I find similarities with most people.

I learned that every time you try a new sport or activity, you should ask the expert three common phrases associated with that sport. That way, when talking to others you sound like you know a lot more.

For example, when I went skydiving, I asked the instructor what terms I should use or not use. Since you can't really talk to the other skydivers while falling, communication is done through body movements. Wiggling your legs quickly back and forth quickly means that you're changing direction. And yelling "geronimo" when about to jump is a common phrase of exhilaration.

Speaking with Cutco experts (Cutco is a professional cooking knife company), I learned the difference between a paring knife used for precision tasks like peeling and making garnishes, a large chef's knife used for cutting and dicing and the santoku knife, which is similar to the chef's knife but more geared towards poultry and fish.

When someone wants to talk about a subject I know nothing about, I take advantage of it and ask them to tell me everything that they know. Boom, the other person is back to talking about themselves, plus they feel special because I've shown interest in something that they like. My typical phrase will be something like, "Wow, I know nothing about [insert topic or activity name], but I want to know more! Could you tell me about it?"

Once I've shown my interest, it's usually easy from there.

I'm bisexual, so have experience with both genders. Whereas there are many similarities between the two (both love sharing stories about themselves), typically it will take a female-identifying individual a few more dates to fall than a male-identifying individual for the deeper connection to happen.

But all comes with practice and patience.

* * *

This next section is definitely the hardest to write.

I've put off writing it for weeks and almost decided to not include it at all. After a chat with my therapist, I decided that it was a topic I needed to include.

Having grown so used to the normal indecencies of machismo and gender inequality around the world, some days, I don't even notice that it is happening anymore.

Things as little as hygiene products. Did you know men's razors cost less than womens'? But more harshly, women are judged negatively for speaking up while it's encouraged for men.

Machismo manifests itself differently in different cultural settings, I've noticed.

I had difficulty justifying the need to include this section and then realized *that* was probably the most important reason I *had* to include it. Women have voices and need to be heard.

Whereas in the liberal California setting, you'd think that you dodged hypocrites, misogyny, and discrimination, you actually face exactly the same barriers.

Things like guys leaving you out of conversations because they're talking about sports. Or "Friday Night with the Boys," which is 100 percent more common in the US than in Latin American communities, where men and women typically enjoy time together in mixed groups.

I came across this beautiful poem by Rupi Kaur that so deeply reflects what our society has valued:

i want to apologize to all the women
i have called pretty.
before i've called them intelligent or brave.
i am sorry i made it sound as though
something as simple as what you're born with
is the most you have to be proud of
when your spirit has crushed mountains
from now on i will say things like "you are resilient"
or, "you are extraordinary."
not because i don't think you're pretty.
but because you are so much more than that

It is so natural to think about a woman's physical appearance before anything else. So much that I end up even modifying parts of myself in order to better appeal to others when my being is gorgeous as it is. If I want to be sexy, it is for me, and if I choose to share it with someone else, that is my decision at that moment.

None of my three parents (mother, father, and stepfather) taught me about feminism.

My mom frequently will make comments that only promote the continuation of the bad mentality.

"I will only ride a girl's bike."

"Don't ask for a raise, that's not professional."

"I want to stop working the minute I hit retirement age."

No wonder women earn less.

My dad doesn't make any comments to my face about women. He's never treated me differently than how I imagine he would've treated a son. (He has three daughters total. I have two half-sisters who were born and raised in Peru before my mom gave birth to me.) My dad teaches me about investments and continued education and constantly improving myself.

However, that luxury is not something practiced with other

women who cross his path, literally.

He catcalls. A lot. And right in front of me. As Rupi Kaur mentioned in her poem, my dad will reduce the value of a woman he sees down to her physical appearance.

He will whistle and tell a girl to come closer. He tells me about their ass and their boobs.

He will tell me how gorgeous she is.

And worst of all, he will tell me how the only reason he wants a woman is so that she can cook, clean, and give him company when he feels he needs it. He wants to go to foreign countries to find a dainty woman, bring her back to America, and be the macho bread winner while she obediently does what he wants, when he wants.

It infuriates me.

We've yelled about it multiple times.

Once on the Strip in Las Vegas crossing the pedestrian bridge in front of the Flamingo Hotel, he started making kissing noises at two other tourists and shouted, "How sexy!"

I lost my shit. I yelled at him right there in front of everyone and stormed away.

Besides embarrassment, I felt ashamed to be even remotely related to someone who would disrespect the body of a woman in such a public manner.

I've seen and experienced much worse myself. But with strangers, it is much easier to ignore. This was someone with whom I was about to dine with on the terrace of Mon Ami Gabi in the Paris Hotel and Casino overlooking the spectacular water show in front of the Bellagio. Chicken liver mousse pâté is just bland, smeary cream next to someone you're not in the mood to enjoy the view with.

My stepfather shows his machismo through very different expressions. He's much quieter than my biological parents. More reserved, keeps to himself. You wouldn't notice it at first sight.

During the pandemic, he lost his job as a shuttle driver. Less travelers, no need to shuttle people.

On top of that, my mom and stepdad had decided in January 2020 to move into my stepdad's apartment and rent out my mom's apartment, meaning that my mom would directly get the extra income.

My mom was the main breadwinner in the house, paid everyone's health insurance, and had passive income from renting her apartment out.

My stepdad's machismo came through quietly. You could tell he lost his sense of "manhood." I should mention, it is for no legit reason. He is still a great person, has great morals, raised me most of my life, has an amazing wife, has a roof over his head and food in the fridge.

He was barely applying to jobs which, granted, annoyed me quite a bit, and I wasn't hushed about it. If you're going to act depress-y but won't do anything to change it, then the problem is you, not society.

One time, as a heartfelt gift, I tried to start a resume for him. To help kick start the application engine. I thought it was nothing but kind. My biological father often asks me to review his LinkedIn profile, emails he is sending out, professional pictures that he is going to use for his business, etc. Just to get someone else's eyes on your work to check is helpful and overall makes you a much stronger candidate. And teamwork always gets you further.

At this point, I had already been out of the house for five years, had been to multiple resume and LinkedIn profile building workshops, had been through countless interview processes and even worked closely with the recruitment team to try to get great candidates for our clients (it was an outsourcing company). If anything, I knew at least a little more than him at this point to have an idea of what employers would look for and how to make the important information stand out.

He never even looked at it. He never even said thank you.

I was destroyed.

A month later, he yelled at me to stay out of his business. I just wanted to help.

My mom told me in private that he was angry at my efforts because he felt emasculated that someone younger than him was trying to give him professional advice. She also mentioned his worry that I was only interested in him getting a job so that he could help pay my student loan, which had never once crossed my mind. I just wanted to support him.

A few months later, my stepdad and I sat down to talk about this specific incident. What I got out of the conversation was that everyone would go his or her own way and not comment on anything that the other person did. Personally, I think that's horrible. Humanity is about being there for others, creating community. My solution at that point, unwillingly, was to stay quiet. Yes, I was pissed and have to admit that I still am. He said to stay out of his business. So, since then we have barely spoken. We never call each other or keep up with each other's lives. I'm not sad anymore, though, because I learned that if someone, even family, doesn't appreciate you, then it's probably better you're not present with them anyway.

Although my parents were not good influences in the terms of machismo, I am still incredibly grateful for them for everything else that they have taught me. Above all, to love. I still love them despite their flaws, and of course, I know I have many, too.

I've also had quite a few machista roommates.

In Peru, I had a roommate who told me I shouldn't be bisexual because men are better at sex and have more to offer. I earned more than him and was independent almost a decade before he was, so what he supposedly had to offer me that was better than a woman confused me.

In Mexico, I lived with an Italian roommate. Although everyone talks about Latin America being extremely "traditional," I have never experienced more machismo than when I was around Italians. I studied in Italy in college. I lived with an Italian family and integrated with the Italian culture on my time out of class. This gave me some first-hand experiences with the culture there, and saw some patterns elsewhere.

My roommate would yell at me for leaving a grain of rice on the stove after cooking, literally! He said that I left the entire place a disaster. Then he would host loud, crowded parties on a Tuesday night, not let me sleep knowing that I had work the next day, and would leave the kitchen filled with 23 bottles of who-knows-what type of alcohol, all the trash bins overflowing, and the entire sink filled with dishes from having fed his invitees.

That particular party got so rowdy that the neighbors complained. The family who lived next door explained that they had an elementary school aged girl who needed to go to school tomorrow. Another neighbor complained that all the cigarettes and ash thrown off the terrace landed on their car.

Once our landlord got word, he informed my roommate that he could get evicted.

This same roommate also left his breakfast dishes in the sink every single morning without washing because he "was in a hurry to get to work." But when I left a plate because I was rushing to get to a class, I was disrupting the environment.

He would speak disrespectfully about women he dated. He would date two or three at a time, and when one didn't want to be with him anymore, he would justify their actions, saying, "Women are crazy and unstable. They are rude and can never be clear."

Sorry, from my understanding the girl was *extremely* clear that she didn't want to be with you.

Also, at one of these parties (at another apartment), another Italian friend of my roommate, who had a girlfriend back in Italy I should mention, aggressively pulled me into a bathroom and tried to undress me.

I pushed him away, but he pulled and continued to try to undress me. He even tried to make a case of how hot it would be to have a threesome with a Canadian chick there.

I continued to push until finally he gave in, and I stormed out of the bathroom, grabbed my jacket, and raced out of the party. I called an Uber on my way down the elevator and hopped in a minute after exiting on the ground floor.

When I tried confessing this to my roommate the next day, I specified that I was just sharing to inform him. My roommate, however, then took it upon himself to try and fix the whole situation by speaking with the other party involved and mentioning that "his friends/roommates" were off limits. Ergo, the actions were okay, just not with close acquaintances because it could cause drama. Thanks. (Not.)

There's also a small list of guys I have dated that go somewhat the opposite way. They promised me the world. They promised to take me on trips, to concerts, to fancy restaurants, to introduce me to their friends. They promised to take me back to their country so I could meet their mom and their dogs. Then, they just fall off the face of the planet.

One guy in particular said he thought of marrying me sometime in the future. Two months later he ghosted me. He reappeared in my life a year and a half later, admitted he had gotten back together with his girlfriend and moved to Argentina to be with her but in the end things didn't work out.

So now he was back, looking for me because he knew I would fall. I did. Again, promise of rings, marriage gowns, inviting all his friends from all over the world to some apparent wedding at an unspecified future date… but he still needed to get over his girlfriend. And then another two months later I got ghosted again.

I felt like a piece of trash. Disposable. He only talked to me when it was convenient emotionally for him. He capitalized on the romance and then disappeared.

I've learned a lot from these situations, though. I need to know how to hold my ground. I've also strengthened my arsenal of emotional tools for use in the future.

* * *

All these incidents have involved me to a certain degree. However, the next story is even more personal.

I've left out names and time-markers. I've replaced most of the places with generic descriptions in order for the people and accounts to remain completely anonymous, as it was my best option at this moment.

I was raped. I wasn't inebriated and I remember the whole scene. For comparison, there was another account of a similar situation that had me equally as stirred for many years before I was able to finally sit down and have a conversation in a calm and non-triggering environment.

The first situation was difficult because I can't quite remember it. I only got details afterwards. I've replaced the person's name with "Person X" for anonymity.

I was at a party with some friends. Some I knew for quite some time, others I had just met that day. The party started in a house, and by midnight or 1:00 AM, the plan was to head out to a club.

By the time we got to the neighborhood famed for parties, the streets were full of people, and there was loud music blasting and drinks being sold throughout the street. There was some sort of big celebration happening that night. It seemed that there was not a soul in his or her house that night.

Whereas I do not party as frequently as others, I was in the mood for a good dance that day.

We danced and we danced, and we drank and we drank. My body was by far not as alcohol tolerant as those of the group I was with; nonetheless I continued to drink and dance the night away. I can barely remember what happened.

My memory is foggy. I only remember some fragments. Here I will detail what I do remember to create a rough summary of the events. I also went back through my journals to piece together some of the details that I don't even remember now, but that I wrote down a few days after.

I was dancing with Person X, and my hand was on his shoulder. My hand accidentally kept pulling down his sleeve, and for the life of me, I could not get it back up because of my inebriation. I remember Person X making a comment on it, but I can't remember what that comment was. The next thing, we were kissing, there in the middle of hundreds of people.

Then Person X backed away, stared at me, and commanded, "You won't forget this right?"

Of course, I said no...

Flash forward to the next thing I remember, I was holding my head trying to think if I was making up what had just happened. We were still at the party but now surrounded again by Person X's friends. I didn't want to make a scene because if it was not true, I would look stupid.

One weird thing about being brownout or blackout drunk—in my cases at least—is that you still remember the emotions you had at the time, just not the scene. I remember feeling confused.

I couldn't see what I was doing.

Somehow later on, we ended up leaving and Person X drove me home. The whole time, Person X kept their hand on my inner thigh. It was 5:30 in the morning at this point, and the sun was already rising.

When I woke up later that day, I had no idea what had happened and it scared me. I had lost complete control.

According to friends who asked about my night, I danced like crazy and then took a taxi home. Simple. Who would ask any questions? Well, no one did; it was that simple.

I wanted to speak to Person X to understand if everything that had happened was real.

We didn't talk at all for a few days, but I finally reached out and asked if we could meet up.

To be honest, I don't know what I wanted to work out. I thought seeing Person X would make me realize that this was all such an unfortunate mishap, and everyone would get over it. Well, Person X got over it, but I did not.

Person X admitted to remembering the whole thing, whereas I couldn't muster up a full sequence of events if my life depended on it.

A few months later, he showed up at my door and proceeded to take my phone out and delete messages that we had exchanged previously in such a way that he seemed we had barely spoken about anything.

I was furious.

I had been taken advantage of.

Above all, I think that's what hurt even more. I had zero power.

Losing complete control was what caused my emotional harm for years to come. And the next incident escalated that situation even more.

In an effort to regain control, a few months later I returned to the street where the situation started. I thought that seeing the area again, sober, would allow me to understand better and maybe spark a memory that would help me piece together my night.

I went, but no new memories came back. Rather, I made up a scene in my head of what it might have looked and felt like that night. Still, I had no power to change it. Just the power to push through.

I was raped. And I was fully conscious. Not a drop of alcohol or anything else in my system. I will refer to the person in this incident as "Person Y" for anonymity.

I'm not afraid or self-conscious about going out by myself. It was a Tuesday night, and after work, I decided to destress at a bar close to my apartment.

I went by myself but ended up running into a group of people

I knew. I chatted with them a bit.

At around 1:00 AM, it was time to walk home.

I lived in an extremely safe neighborhood, so walking alone at that time of the night was also completely safe.

As I was walking out, Person Y came running after me. He grabbed me by the hips and pulled me close to him.

I pushed him away playfully, somewhat joking around because I, of course, didn't think anything big of the situation yet.

He teased me about leaving so soon when everyone else was still having fun.

It was obvious as of a few months prior that Person Y was interested in me, at least physically. He seemed to get jealous when I was in the company of other people who were flirting with me. However, it was never brought up explicitly.

(I should mention that this person and I had been intimate a few times previously but were never in any sort of relationship. Person Y and I just ran into each other frequently by accident because our friends ran in the same circles.)

That night, Person Y pushed me against the wall of the building and begged me to let him take me home. Person Y had a car, which suspiciously and conveniently was right where we were standing that point.

Although the walk home was only about 20 minutes and I'm not one to be lazy about walking, I was a bit cold and didn't think anything of Person Y dropping me off in front of my building. I confided in him. I accepted.

As we got closer to the entrance to my building, suddenly he made a turn down the street one block from my place.

"You know my apartment building is straight, not to the right," I stated.

"I know," he replied with a sly grin on his face.

This was the point where I started getting a little bit suspicious about his intentions, but since we had been intimate prior, I wasn't completely opposed to it potentially happening again. This is where a strong consent mentality comes in.

Just because a girl wears tight clothing, looks at you in a "provocative" way, even kisses you, and above all, invites you to her house, that is not an *automatic* motion of consent. Consent has to be received every single time you want to have sexual intercourse. It doesn't matter if you are just friends, a couple, new acquaintances, etc. All sex should be consensual.

Person Y walked me to the door of my building and pulled me into an even tighter embrace while kissing me. I tried to push away again saying that I had to sleep because I had to work the next day.

Person Y did not care.

He took my keys and opened the doors himself.

In the elevator on the way up to my floor, he tried to undress me. I was reasonably smaller and less muscular than Person Y, but at that point, I still managed to push him off, saying that there was no way anything would happen in a public space.

We got to my apartment door. Person Y opened the door and let himself in. He grabbed my hand and led me down the hallway to my bedroom.

The second the door to my bedroom closed, everything changed.

Person Y pushed me, hard. I fell against my light pink sheets, knocking my calf against the bed frame on my way down.

I turned around quickly to face him.

"You think you can get away from me?!" he blared.

It sunk in that he was not just a normal level of jealous. He was angry, feisty, and out for revenge for me "letting" other men flirt and/or be with me.

He wanted me for himself and did NOT like sharing.

I laid on the bed for a split second, shocked, before his next move.

He approached me, and in one pull, my pants and underwear

were thrown to the other side of the room. He unbuckled his pants and lowered them to his mid-thigh.

Without any time for natural lubrication, he penetrated me, hard and fast. I tried to squirm out from underneath his weight with no avail.

He pounded harder and harder.

At one point, he picked me up, ripped off my shirt, and turned me over.

He began spanking me aggressively. I screamed for him to stop, that I was in pain. I tried reaching my hand back to intercept the next blow from making contact with my backside.

He ejaculated quickly. Just a few minutes of hard and sandpaper-y seeming penetrative sex later.

He fell down on top of me and grabbed my left wrist. Holding my wrist, he slapped himself across *his* face with *my* hand.

"I shouldn't have done that," he confessed coldly. He stood up and zipped up his pants. "I'll let myself out." And he was gone.

I was still lying naked on my bed. Still in shock. Everything had happened so quickly.

At this point, it was around 2:00 AM on a Wednesday morning. No one should have been awake. I decided to message my friend anyway, and surprisingly, she responded.

"I think I was just raped." That's how I opened the conversation.

I never cried. I never went to get rape tested in the morning. I was in complete shock. How could this happen to *me*?

And he *knew* what he was doing.

After a few days, I decided I wanted to do something about it. I was not going to be left without control. I wanted to report him. I wanted him in jail. I hated him. I couldn't stand him.

I went to the police department, but later that afternoon when I was scheduled to see a lawyer specialized in abuse cases, I couldn't bring myself to report.

I explained the entire story. Every detail. And then she told me that with everything I had to present, he would go to jail for six years and have the sexual assault on his record for life.

I wanted it, and *still* want that so bad. But I couldn't do it. Something held me back. And I still don't know what.

The social fear? The personal fear? I can't quite tell.

Another week passed, and I didn't go back to the police office yet. At this point, it was too late to get rape tested because all the semen in my vagina would have already been absorbed. I did go to get STI tested though, just in case.

I met up with a friend and shared with her what had happened. She was one of the most supportive people I could have told. I told her my fears, and she said that she would return with me to the police office to report him.

It was around 9:00 PM. She googled the closest office from where we were chatting, and we walked there together. I, again, told the representative my story, and she wrote everything down. She again offered me the option to commence the legal process and get Person Y in jail as quickly as possible.

And then…something held me back again.

To this day, I cannot describe the exact emotion going through my mind at that moment. Numbness is probably the most accurate.

I didn't report.

But, I decided *not* to keep my mouth shut in social circles.

Perhaps my reason for sharing in this book, sharing with the world, and sharing my story with those around me is to bring more light to the fact that it DOES happen way more often than you'd imagine. And yes, it happens with people you know. Not just a random person who saw you in a restaurant with your friends.

I confronted him the next time I saw him in person and told him that he raped me. As expected, he denied it. Everything.

I began to tell everyone, not that he was a rapist, but that they should be careful.

I played the inverse psychology card.

"Oh my, you like him? I've had sex with him. Good in bed, but oh my, he's with six people at a time, always. After I figured that out, I had to get an STI test. Have your fun but be careful."

It worked. Not one of the people ended up with him.

So much so, that all the sudden, he started noticing is lack of sexual wins and finally someone accidentally let it slip that I had said something.

I was walking out of a grocery store with my hands full of grocery bags one Saturday afternoon when I got a call from him.

"Do you have time to talk?"

At this point, I didn't know that word had gotten around to him. But he was clearly affected because it's not something that dies down quickly. He lost all potential sexual gain on almost any girl. His ego was hit, and that's what hurt him most.

I ended up hanging up and calling him back when I was at a place where I could put down my bags.

"You told Girl X to be careful with me! Why does it matter to you who I'm with or not? Just stay out of it."

"Excuse me? You raped me!"

And that's when, again, the threats began. He threatened to report ME to the police for defamation. That's how much he thought his reputation was affected.

Good thing for me, everything I had told everyone was true, and defamation can only ever be confirmed if the statements someone shared were *not* true, with the specific intention of ruining his or her social status. All my statements were true.

During that call, he used every psychological trick he knew. I'm not going to lie, it worked. He threatened me with his money, power, and connections in the police department. He said he'd take legal action against anything I tried to do from there on out. He said that he'd be my worst nightmare.

I was scared.

Not just because someone who used to be my friend had changed, but because all of a sudden, I was at the mercy of being reported the other way around.

All the sudden, I found myself not only a victim of rape, but a victim of heavy threats.

I called the police office as soon as I got home, and it turned out there was nothing illegal about what I had done. I, of course, would have used that in the conversation with Person Y had I known, but I figured it out too late.

The biggest regret I have is having forgotten to record the conversation.

I was in a legal position that he should have been in. All the sudden, I felt like I had to protect myself legally, instead of *him* protecting himself from the abuse he committed. He turned everything around. He manipulated me.

I was scared.

I called the police hotline back to see what I could do in the event that I had been threatened, even though I was the victim.

How could this happen to me?

I *hated* him. I couldn't stand him. I was so mad, I couldn't even cry. I was fuming, and it was just building stronger and stronger by the minute.

At moments like these, I typically go running or to the gym. Movement helps me get out of a bad emotional state. This time, I couldn't. I just laid in bed. I didn't cry. I let my mind go blank.

I ran into Person Y again a few days later. We didn't talk, but I saw him with another girl. I already knew he was always with five or six girls at a time. Unbelievable. I heard about some of the other girls and how they had been either heartbroken or emotionally hurt by him. It was a trend.

But this new girl, she was different. She was SO young. You could tell. Ridiculously young. Not just from the way she looked physically, but the way she acted. It was confirmed later on that I was right, she was WAY young.

That was where I emotionally could not take it anymore.

He had hurt someone who was emotionally independent and who had a usually strong character. I knew those individuals would be able to survive. Also, at least push him off a little. These girls had already developed their mechanisms of emotional defense to a strong enough level.

I was not able to push him off physically, but this girl, she was a toothpick; even I could pick her up. If he wanted to, he could squash her.

That was my ultimate tipping point.

That's the first time I cried. Not because of jealousy, but because of fury towards the devastating situation that this girl was in, and she had no idea. She was so innocent.

My friend eventually ended up confronting both of them, Person Y and the new girl, at a party one night. My friend told the girl what an asshole Person Y was and is.

The girl was already brainwashed by this point.

"Get over it, you're just jealous."

I COULDN'T BELIEVE IT!

In my mind, she was already lost. He already got to her.

I started sharing more of my pain with other people. I shifted to more of a heartfelt, painful feeling for the girl.

Worst, I must say, his threats actually worked in altering my overall behavior.

Then I started getting the comment, "You have to learn how to forgive yourself to get over him." I hated that. I, of all people, had to forgive *myself*. Excuse me, for what?! WHAT THE FUCK!

After my friend confronted him and the girl, he sent me one last message basically to fuck off, even though I hadn't said anything. That was the last interaction we had.

In both situations, I felt I had completely lost control. I tried to regain control by confronting both other people, but in both situations it didn't help. Whether that was a good idea or not, I am not sure.

I still have not decided if it was a good idea not to report, but I know that my reasons for choosing that path are now at least clearer.

Who would a judge and jury believe me? A young woman fighting for her right to be heard, or a man who says that the girl is just overreacting because she's heartbroken and who doesn't have any evidence to prove her statements?

My purpose is to share my stories with others so that others can make better decisions that then make changes in the system.

The change is not to encourage people, predominantly young females, to dress in more conservative clothing or to not go out alone. It is to encourage our society to teach everyone to NOT rape. In fact, I continue to dress in shorts and a sports bra or a small top. In a way I feel this helps me gain control over my body by dressing as I please but now being stronger when I'm not comfortable, at the first sight of a situation going wrong.

My purpose is not to put individuals in jail, and although I may believe they should be, I am more interested in educating people about the topic. I was informed that even if the trial process got started, it could be anywhere from six months to two years of constantly having to be in court. This would have implied a constant emotional toll on me, time spent not growing professionally, potentially losing my job, the possibility of not winning anyway, and much more. I knew I could better spend my time, energy and emotions elsewhere. And that is what I did. Here I am making a much bigger impact, on more than just one person.

I realized that my happiness would not increase by continuing the legal process.

At first it felt like I was giving up and that he had won. To this day, I still have moments when I feel like his threats are controlling me from afar and that angers me. However, I know that I made the decision based on what was best for my life at that moment.

I am here to give light to the situation and find and demonstrate ways that others can avoid these situations, protect themselves afterwards and teach our society not to rape. Period.

CHAPTER 6

An Afterthought

A myth some might believe is that bipolar symptoms come in predictable waves. It doesn't. Situations can definitely influence and provoke either a manic or depressive episode. It's clear that these situations did not leave me excited for anything. Quite the opposite.

I didn't want anything to do with anyone for months afterwards.

I still grapple with the idea frequently. Whenever someone makes a negative comment about females, degrades them down to their body image, or calls them emotional and not apt for work I get frustrated. I hate it.

Self-help books help. Stories like *The 5AM Club* by Robin Sharma really spoke to me. At the end, the protagonists visit the jail cell that Nelson Mandela was locked in for 30 years.

Nelson Mandela was urinated on, spat on, starved, beat, frozen, and more.

Upon walking out of the jail cell, he forgave each and every one of his abusers. He looked them in the eyes and forgave them.

He was free. Both physically and mentally. He let go, and that's powerful. To have the power to say that someone else is no longer in charge of your life is impressive.

No one can change the world until they learn to forgive. Not forget but forgive.

Remembering is a good thing. It keeps you alert to future

dangers. But that past can't be changed, only grappled with.

I'm not there yet. I see the power of it and have already begun to heal so many of my emotional wounds, but I haven't quite made it yet. I'm on my own path. Therapy helps, no doubt. So does getting involved in other personal projects. But I'm not there yet.

Dear reader, I appreciate your comprehension. And if you ever would like to vent about your personal situation, please feel free to reach out to me personally.

CHAPTER 7

Diets I've Tried

Let's move on to a topic a little more lovely.

I have tried SOOOOOO many diets.

My conclusion: They ALL work. The biggest thing about trying different diets is that you have to have the right mindset. You have to fully be IN it. These days, cheat meals are commonly accepted or even encouraged in diets in order to curb cravings, so there's not even the need to worry about missing out on your chocolate fudge cake or Friday night beer.

My obsession with health and exercise started in high school and has had a major positive impact on my mood swings and dealing with bipolar.

I was a cheerleader in high school. Not just a sideline cheerleader, but a competitive cheerleader. I loved it. I love being in front of people.

Stage fright? I don't have it. I can walk up on a stage and not have a damned clue about what I will do and not be embarrassed. This flows well with my "I" personality type from the DISC profile. That's not a promise that I will do anything cool. I probably couldn't put on a comedy show, but I damn sure will try. I can dance. No singing. Definitely no singing. But I would feel totally comfortable with the eyes of an audience on me.

Sideline cheerleading was great for that.

Competitions were even better. High energy, cute makeup,

and an extremely physically demanding sport. I loved every moment of cheer and cheer practice. I loved the family I had. And when traveling the world after college, I always looked up cheer teams in the cities I would be in and tried to work out with them. It was great getting to learn and share new techniques across the globe.

I ended up competing in the Panamerican international cheer competition in Peru, representing Peru in 2018. We landed second place, enough to get us into the international competition in Japan. I couldn't go, but members from my team went to represent.

I started working out heavily because of cheer. I had jogged slightly before but had no structured routines or schedules.

In college, I racked up a great workout routine in the small gym in the basement of my freshman dorm building.

"Gym" might be an exaggeration of the word. The "gym" had one elliptical, one smith machine, and one bicycle. And a little bit of open space. It was sad, but it was enough for at least 30 minutes of consistent movement on busy days, and one hour on more lax days.

My body got into a great routine.

Keeping a steady workout routine helps to stabilize emotions. I use it in lieu of medicating.

Personally, I don't medicate. It is really up to each individual and the strength of his or her manic and depressive episodes. Your environment may influence your decision one way or the other, but it is important to know what works for you.

It's a matter of trial and error. I tried lithium, which is the go-to medication for bipolar people. Because of the nature of bipolar, antidepressants will shock the person into a manic episode while antipsychotics or depressants will cause a depressive episode. Lithium is a mood stabilizer. Works for some. I HATED it. It made me basically feel like a potato. I wasn't happy nor sad, enthused nor turned off, motivated nor unmotivated. I was just a blop.

Exercise and eating healthy is the other option that mental health experts typically suggest.

Starting with cheer, I learned what working out hard meant.

Feeding your body foods rich in healthy nutrients also gives your brain the power to manage emotions better, so I started testing different diets.

I have tried:
- Intermittent Fasting
- Carb cycling
- Carb counting/low carb
- Marco counting
- Keto
- Vegetarianism
- Veganism
- Starving (unfortunately, and I hated this one, not recommended)
- Paleo
- Low fat
- Gluten-free
- Lactose-free

Some were for weight loss, some for weight gain, some just to try, and others because my environment made it seem like a good idea at the time. For example, my freshman year college roommate went vegan, so I thought to try it, too.

I come back to old diets once in a while and try them again. They still work, as long as I put my mind to them, but I definitely cannot stick to just one. I either get too bored or too antsy.

Or get fully invested in a new one that seems wayyy more interesting because new studies came out about it, and I want to try it again. Newsflash: same results.

Overall, most diets all work, per my experience. Diet-ING for me is difficult for more than two weeks. I just sustain an overall healthy intake of food.

I've also trained myself to crave healthy foods.

One day, I was reading about brainwashing and manipulation.

Our brains can be rewired. I thought that was crazy…and then realized that I could try and use it to my benefit. The result was me rewiring my cravings. It works!

If you're interested in doing the same, just jot down what you've eaten and how you feel two to three hours after every meal or snack for two weeks or three. Looking back, you will notice you feel better after having eaten healthy, nutritious food, and you will naturally start to look for more of it. Kind of like a drug, but a good one.

Be strict with yourself at the beginning, and then you will realize that your body naturally wants to feel energized, awake, and present.

Similarly, after years of practice, I have instilled the necessity in myself to workout.

Every single day, I do something active. Usually, it is just simple workouts using the weights, bands, and blocks I bought for my apartment. Some days I will pay the one-day entrance fee for the gym or go with a friend who has a membership and can give me a free visitor pass.

Other days, I'll go on a hike or something else outside, like a water sport.

Since I am naturally more on the hyperactive side, I get a lot of energetic and emotional stability from intense physical movement or physical stress; for example, when I choose to lift heavy weights.

I also had to test out a lot of my workout routines.

I love yoga, but I can't do a full hour more than once per week, if at all. It can get extremely intense depending on the level class I take and the instructor. However, I lean towards a preference of high cardio and heavy weight activities that can put my physical strength and endurance to the test.

That being said, I still meditate every day, which is the grounding activity after my exercise.

I've also tried two small workouts per day, or skipping one

day in between, or giving myself one to two "cheat days" per week. For me personally, none of those have worked out as well as just getting my ass up every day and moving.

I also sign up for various classes at the gym. I love the social aspect and the consistency, and commitment definitely helps me mentally.

I've tried body pump, functional, cross fit, Zumba, salsa workout, spin/cycle, yoga, hot yoga, pole dancing, reggaeton dance, heels, boxing, midnight runners and probably some other ones that I cannot remember at the moment. I have been arooouuunnnddd!

Okay, so what?? Why is this all so important?

My superpower, being bipolar, gave me the initial curiosity to try one diet after another. In the end, it gave me a more expansive and personal knowledge on what each diet was like. I also tried a variety of different physical workout types to see which best fits my character.

Few other people are inclined, interested, or even have the patience to go through one trial period after another year in and year out. I was trying something new every month. Some months, I would go back and try a workout style or diet I had tried four months ago to test it out again. Then back to the cycle. Also, I needed to combine different workouts with different types of diets to see what was working best. Keto diet while on a mostly dance and cardio workout schedule was not good for my body type. Carb cycling and cross fit made me bulk up, and quick. It was trial and error.

By not adhering to what society expected, I now have more connections with a wider variety of people because I can speak personally to others that have each tried different types of diet and exercise routines.

In my mind, this puts me above others. After all, I do have my superpower, so I cannot complain.

CHAPTER 8

Proactivity

People with bipolar (I know this from being one, having lived with one, and also having researched things that I have done) tend to start a lot of tasks but don't end up finishing them.

"People with bipolar disorder appear to value goal pursuit more than do other people," says Sheri L. Johnson, a professor at the University of California, Berkeley, whose work has focused on bipolar disorder.

I must admit, starting projects is fun. And I identify highly with the above quote.

My personality is naturally very optimistic, which leads me to think that everything I set my mind to will end up amazing.

Take an online course? This will supplement my LinkedIn profile and my resume, and there is NO WAY that an employer would dare not hire me.

Take a dance class? I will be SO SEXY afterwards that any girl or guy looking at me will IMMEDIATELY fall in love. How could they not?

Make an amazing positive, uplifting poster that I will hang in my room? There is NO WAY that I will EVER feel down again. Impossible. Because I'll have a poster that says positive things (spoiler: things don't work like that, but the positivity definitely helps).

Designing projects for me is great. Looking at the big picture, figuring out how it will all fit into the grander scheme of my life.

Researching the details of how that specific project (self-project or class) will benefit me or change an aspect of my perception for the better. I love it.

Following through, however, is a different story. Call it motivation or whatever you want. I have issues following through.

I can't help it. I get BORED!

This may also be very common in people without bipolar. Once they figure out the issues involved in completing the project, they get demotivated and/or distracted with other life events. Dealing with solving the issue is too much stress compared to the benefit that would potentially be received.

(Speaking of getting demotivated and distracted, I just left that previous paragraph half-finished to go to the kitchen refrigerator and grab myself a delicious macaron that I bought from *Le Macaron French Pastries* in the *Shoppes* section of the Venetian Hotel in Las Vegas. I'm currently on another trip visiting my dad in Vegas and have made it tradition to always stop by The Venetian for a pastry. My favorite Vegas hotel and my favorite pastry. Okay, that's my distraction moment, back to writing now…)

(Never mind—I have another interjection. My dad just came flying out of his home office to tell me about an amazing idea he had. He wants to teach me about project risk and project stress analysis. Weird how well that fits in with the thought I just finished adding to this book. I'm intrigued and will continue that conversation with him later today because I have dedicated 6:00 AM to 11:00 AM today to just writing.)

Anyway, back to the quote at the top of this section.

Bipolar people value *the pursuit*. If you've ever listened to any motivational speaker or read essentially any self-help or life motivation book by almost any author, be it a classic like *As a Man Thinketh* or *Rich Dad, Poor Dad* or something more like *Good to Great*, then you will have read about valuing the present moment more than absolutely anything else.

You can't live in future events. You can only manifest them based on your actions today.

You can't literally relive the past. Flashbacks and some sorts of stress disorders make you *feel* like you're back there, but you are here. You are in the present. You can only change your actions and emotions now.

So being present for the *pursuit* of your goal is the ultimate summit.

And bipolar people, like myself, are naturally there. Superpower? I. Think. Yes!

After all, ridiculously successful people all seem to have a little something that makes them a little "crazy" (read: different). I say superhuman, but interpret as you wish.

Being bipolar is great. I am naturally fit to think the way highly successful people recommend the average Joe should think.

If the project doesn't pan out the way I originally planned, well, at least I gave it a shot, and I most likely learned something new—both from my previous research and from my personal intent to complete it.

A quite peculiar way that I believe I am proactive is with my emotions. I purposefully put myself into tough situations in order to get out of them quickly. Think of it as the philosophy of "failing fast" in order to get to your desired outcome quicker.

I've hit "rock bottom" probably more times than most. I would argue that most people will hit a depression point once, maybe twice in their lives. This is when they feel they've lost everything, have nowhere to go and don't belong anywhere. Their lives seem stagnant in relation to the moving parts around them.

These big points are typically referred to as either a quarter life crisis or a midlife crisis. Sound familiar?

I would argue that I've hit a similar "bottom" much more frequently. I'm experienced enough to now use them to my benefit and purposely place myself in more of a "pressure cooker" of emotions in order to come out more quickly.

Do I want to be sad? No, not particularly.

I don't sit around at home, saying, "I'm bored, let me just be sad to kick start my swing," or "I'm having writer's block, so let me induce depression real quick to get out of this cycle."

No; definitely no.

But when an impactful event happens, I know that letting myself cry until I'm a raisin and spending two days without leaving my apartment will put me in a stage of "get your f***ing sh*t together."

For example, I lost a big contract with an Australian-based contract since they decided they no longer wanted to have operations in the US.

The afternoon after my direct boss and the CEO of the company shared this news with me, I huddled up in a ball on my mattress on the floor (I had not yet purchased a bed frame in the new apartment I was living in) and wept.

I had anticipated the company moving in a different direction for a few weeks. The company was shifting from what it had been when I originally came on board, but I tried to hold on as long as I could.

After getting the official notice and sharing the news with my therapist, she informed me that every loss or change is perceived differently depending on what happens afterwards.

For example, if a romantic relationship ends and you end up with someone better (using whatever personal criteria you have for determining that), then you will perceive the end of the first relationship as a positive change that allowed you the space and emotional availability to accept a new person in your life (well, considering you were not unfaithful to begin with, but you get the point).

However, if the first relationship ends and then you are either unwillingly single—which I argue is actually a positive, but to everyone his/her own opinion—or start a toxic relationship with someone who sucks money out of you and destroys you emotionally, then you will perceive the end of the first relationship as perhaps the most devastating event to have happened to you.

The most important mentality to have after an unwanted event happens to you is to do everything in your power to make the next step in your life better than the preceding one.

Regarding this loss, there were a few options that came to mind. I could take things slows by taking a sabbatical and travel to Indonesia to add more cultural richness to my persona (or any other country I didn't know at the time). Or find a different project to work on. Or just relax for a bit and explore the city I lived in more, which was Mexico City at the time. Or open a new business. Soon I saw my opportunities were endless.

I opted for a mixture of traveling and working on myself. In this case, working on myself meant opening up my own business, reading a lot, and finishing writing my book.

After balling up, crying, thinking I was useless, jobless, and going nowhere, I booked a trip to Veracruz, a port city on the Mexican Gulf coast of Mexico for one week to get away. Being there, I organized my next steps.

I would spend a heavy amount of time on my book (the one you are reading right now) and start submitting it to publishers. I had always wanted to write but never gave myself enough time to sit and finish my manuscript.

I opened up a business that continues to function today and provides e a nice source of passive income monthly, on top of being an independent contractor for another business.

Thinking positively, all of a sudden, I was given enough time to focus on writing and polishing my work. Not a lot of other people get that luxury. I just turned a negative into a positive.

I was already accustomed to the ups and downs of bipolar. I was emotionally prepared to take a hit and know that afterwards I would get right back up again and find a new path.

How many others have that superpower? Not many, I can tell you that. But there is a lesson here for everyone to learn, not just other bipolar people. Feeling depressed, lost, scared, disoriented, or a mixture of all those emotions isn't necessarily the worst thing that could happen to you.

Use your depression as a wakeup call to change something. If you're uncomfortable, your body is telling you to switch things up. It's telling you that you need something more or different. That is something very natural.

Naturally, my superpower gave me a base that influencers across the board advocate for. I am extremely thankful for my superpower!

CHAPTER 9

Being Bisexual

I am bisexual. I like men and women. I have no particular incline toward one or the other. I value personality most of all, and everything else comes second.

I am extremely lucky to be in a family that accepts me. I fully understand that that is not the case for most, and more so for people who come from a Latin American family, as Latin Americans tend to be more traditionally religious.

At 19, when I told my mom I was dating a girl, she promptly responded with:

"I knew it!"

On that same trip back home, I told my stepdad, who calmly just said, "Oh okay, did you tell your mom?"

My dad was a different case. He had berated me with hatred towards gays since I was young. He was raised and bred in a strong Catholic household that not only disrespected the LGBT community but also preached saving sex for marriage. Lol. Yeah, not my lifestyle.

Why did I feel the need to tell him? Most suggested I just keep it to myself. What he doesn't know doesn't hurt him. And it's not like I even lived in the same city as him, so he would never accidentally see me walking around holding hands with a woman. I wanted to tell him because I do not like keeping things from my dad. If he was going to show me his love, I wanted it to be for the full me, not just a fraction.

Being bisexual, or even if I was lesbian or transsexual or anything else on the LGBTQIA+ scale, I was only expressing love and being myself. None of these gender or sexual identities puts anyone else in harm's way. I wasn't stealing or killing or cheating or anything else. I was loving.

So yes, I wanted to share with my dad.

(Side note: I recently read an article, TBD if the fact is true or not, that now straight people have STDs at a higher rate than homosexuals. Not sure how that whole issue is going to go with gays being forbidden from donating blood. I'd like to see health organizations ban straight people from donating.)

At the time, my dad was living in the Bay Area. For a routine visit, I flew into SFO on a Friday night to see him and stay the weekend.

He picked me up from the curb, and we agreed that hunger was the primary concern at the moment, so we took a pit stop at a sushi place on the way back to his apartment.

We ordered edamame as an appetizer and red dragon rolls to fill us up.

The closer we got to the end of the roll, the more nervous I got. I didn't want to wait any longer.

"Papi, I need to tell you something," I stuttered.

"Sure, go ahead."

I lost it. I started crying. I hadn't even started talking yet. The tears rolled down my red and puffing cheeks as I tried to grasp for air.

"What's wrong?" my dad asked. "Is everything alright?"

"I like guys *and* girls." That was all I could get out. No further explanation. Although I had thought of telling him for quite some time, I had never actually practiced what I was going to say, ironically.

Here is where everything took a turn that I was not expecting.

After years of saying that homosexuals are horrible and are the causes of diseases in this world and God doesn't want them and a million other hateful comments, my dad responded with:

"Why are you crying about that? I like girls, too. Now we have something else in common." And smiled.

WHAT?!

Did MY DAD really just say that we now have something else in common?? I'm bisexual! He's straight!

My face went blank. How was this possible?

I was quiet. *Okay*, I thought, *this is actually probably the best response I could have received from him. Be happy, Karina, this is awesome.*

I let the last of my tears dribble down my now shocked face. We stood up and gave each other a huge hug.

Once outside the restaurant, we hugged again, one of those huge, tight hugs that seems to last a lifetime. I admit I cried again.

Later on, my dad and I chatted more about the topic, and he confessed to having a change of heart much before I shared my personal situation with him.

My dad proved to me here—and has in other moments as well—that people can change. Educating yourself on new topics, reading, watching videos, and interacting with groups that think differently than you help you grow.

It's okay to change your mind. And it's necessary for growth.

Being bipolar, I change my mind frequently. It's natural. My superpower here? That I learned to accept it. Change is growth. I'm not moving backwards; I'm improving and adjusting both my actions and mentality constantly, depending on new input that I get from my environment. I never seem to go backwards though. Always forward. Focusing on the present and the most that I can give in that moment.

The rest of my family was generally extremely supportive. Aunts, uncles, cousins, even family friends. My grandmother was the only person who was not on board with the idea.

Per a book I read sometime last year (I cannot remember the name of it), bisexual people are the most misunderstood group of the LGBT community. If the bisexual person is with a same-sex partner, then others will say they are either gay or lesbian without taking into consideration that one or both people may identify as bisexual.

Similarly, if others perceive an opposite gendered couple, there will be no doubt they will think it is a standard heterosexual relationship, no questions asked.

My grandmother was similarly confused and not content with her confusion when I told her.

"But which gender do you like more?" and "Have you had sex with both? With which do you feel more pleasure?" were her questions.

Not sure why that mattered. (I know most are probably curious about the answer, too, and my answer is that anyone can make me cum depending on the effort that he or she puts in.) It really shouldn't matter to my grandma whether I cum or not with one gender or the other.

She ended up crying by the end of the conversation. Mainly because of confusion, I'm assuming.

The main message I got was "if you were lesbian, it would have been easier." But if I would have said I was lesbian, I'm sure she would have wanted me to be "half straight," as many people in her generation think of bisexuals as.

As mentioned earlier, we really just ignore the topic completely. She specified that she doesn't want me to present any romantic partners to her. I respect her just to not cause more drama.

CHAPTER 10

Work Life

The pandemic did nothing but good for my professional career. That sounds horrible, I know. But hear me out.

Did the pandemic do good for society? That's up for interpretation.

Personally, being indecisive about where I want to live meant that being remote offered me probably the best option for what I wanted to do in my life.

I was already working remotely for one year before the pandemic started, but that company was one of very few willing to hire a 22-year-old with no prior remote experience. I must say, I felt lucky when I hit that jackpot, but I also knew that I was *not* going to accept *any* work contract unless it was remote, even if I was being paid shit (which I was, but better shit than my job before that, which was more shit, so it seemed good at the time, in comparison).

When the pandemic hit and everyone started working from home, nothing changed for me. At home set up, check. Workout routine, check. Ability to roll out of bed and be mentally ready for a conference call 10 minutes later, check. Ability to stay away from scouring the kitchen and fridge every 15 minutes, check.

When I needed to switch jobs in order to not get paid less than minimum wage, asking for a remote position was just that much easier. (For your understanding, I was getting paid a flat fee of two grand a month, which technically was enough in Latin America, but while staying in San Diego, I couldn't even pay rent, so I slept on a mattress on the floor in my parents' apartment). All companies now understood that a remote set-up was feasible, and work could still be done at or sometimes at a better quality than before. Also, a shift from hourly-based work to a base salary seemed to take place across the board in companies internationally. As long as the worker met his or her KPIs for the week, month, or year, it really didn't matter if they were online for exactly eight hours Monday through Friday or not. This came with the downside of having to connect on the weekends or holidays if you could not finish the work during the week.

To be honest, sometimes I worked on Sundays and then gave myself the luxury of taking half of the following Friday off. Or I would not schedule meetings until 2:00 PM on a Tuesday to go have brunch with friends but then work till 10:00 PM. I loved my setup. And I continue to love it.

With my laptop in my backpack, I connected from wherever I was. Be it the beach in Playa del Carmen—a small town in between Cancun and Tulum—a farm in Valle de Bravo—a small city four hours out of Mexico City—Puerto Rico, Fort Lauderdale, Washington D.C., Peru, etc. I once even spent eight hours in the Houston airport working before my flight, in the United terminal at the restaurant that has the best airport ribs you can find! Extra barbeque sauce, please.

I was able to cure my bug for movement and adventure while simultaneously advancing my professional career the way I wanted.

Bipolarity makes me feel good about a city for a while, and seven to eight months later, I get bored. By acknowledging this aspect up front and not trying to push it down, I can focus on the opportunities that will benefit my personal situation and choose to completely ignore anything that is not in line with what I'm looking for.

I have worked in an office before, and it is not for me. I'm the stereotypical "water cooler girl." I stand by the water cooler all day long and wait for people to fill up their water bottles or glasses and tell me about the drama in their life. If my time there gets too suspicious, I go to the bathroom for a while. And since I was drinking a huge amount of water already, I had lots of liquid to expose at a high frequency. Bathroom chats? Yes, please.

Although it may not look good on a resume, I have also switched jobs quite frequently for my age. Which actually is not as bad as it may seem.

I've had four jobs in the past five years. If you do the math, that means that I switch jobs on average every 1.25 years. Not the best record. I'm extremely professional, diligent, present, and punctual with each of my companies while I'm with them, but nothing big outside of that.

I get bored or see a better opportunity or stop being the top employee, as bubbly or some other combination of a slacker. The time with my employers has gotten longer, though, as I am learning how to diversify my involvement within the same company in order to grow from within.

When I interview for new jobs, I explain that I was looking for more growth or a similar topic. Which is completely the truth. I don't lie, I must say. I am merely fanciful with the way I choose to word my answers to difficult questions.

But also, so what if I haven't stayed in a job for three years? I'm in my twenties and am experimenting with new environments and activities.

This all came to my benefit once I realized that doing whatever was best for myself set me up for the best success because I was and am naturally more motivated to execute my plans.

When I quit my office job to go remote at the beginning of 2019, obviously I did not foresee a global pandemic hitting in 2020; I just wanted to work from wherever I wanted. Well, badaboom; pandemic hits, and I'm already one year into no commutes, signing in online, and understanding Zoom meeting functions.

Apart from that, during my early career, being in multiple different companies has offered me the opportunity to see how different organizations work. There are various ways to come to conclusions about certain problems and various ways to solve one problem. Sometimes my boss at one company was not aware of a platform that was used in another company and sometimes I got to learn about something new.

Cross-pollinating gave me a more diverse set of professional tools and experiences to understand different departments and workflows.

By the time I was 25, I had already worked with one mid-sized company, one huge international company, and two start-ups. I knew how to use HubSpot Marketing and Sales tools, NetSuite, SuiteApps, and more CRM tools. I was educated in international financing tools as well as cross-border contracting and compliance laws. From personal experience, I understood the pain points in start-ups as well as thousand-people-big, multi-national corporations. I could more easily interact with tiny businesses and set them up for success if they wanted to adopt tendencies that bigger corporations were already using. I became an asset.

I have friends who stayed with the same company from the time they graduated college for the following six years.

There are benefits to that as well, of course. You have a greater understanding of the single organization and have seen the department in high and low points. You probably know the HR lady by her first name, how many kids she has, and have her number in your phone.

Sure, I'd like that sometimes. But there is no negative in the way I decided to manage my life either.

Potentially most interesting to most readers is the huge financial benefit, at least in my experience, from switching jobs early in your career.

According to Daniel Pink in his book *When: The Scientific*

Secrets of Perfect Timing, the higher the salary of the individual at the beginning of his or her professional career, the higher salary he or she ends with at the end of life.

Since we expect promotions year after year and from one job to another, someone who already starts out at a higher level will naturally be taking steps from a higher rung on the financial ladder.

Someone who starts lower will ask for a raise respectively of the lower salary that he or she is making. For example, someone looking for a five to ten percent raise on a 40K base income will still be making less than someone looking for a five to ten percent raise on a 60K income.

I switched around a lot and am currently earning at least $20K more per year than the friends that I graduated high school and college with. $20,000. Imagine what you could buy (read: invest in) using 20 extra grand.

To put in perspective, at the time of writing this book, minimum wage in my home state of California is $15/hour. A full-time job at that rate would yield $29,340/year. $20,000 extra is 66% of that.

(Extra tip: I always use glassdoor.com before going into interviews to see what the position with my experience level and expertise is worth. My negotiation does not use the words "I'm asking for" but rather "in line with market value, this position is priced at a range between X and Y dollars per year. This is in line with my salary expectation." Feel free to use that as many times as you need. If your potential future employer is not willing to pay on market, then (a) they are assholes, and you just proved to them that you know they're assholes; and (b) you shouldn't want to work with them anyway.)

Inflation is another aspect to keep in mind.

Inflation, it's a thing. Stop being scared of it and face it head on. There's something called COLA. It stands for Cost Of Living Adjustment. If your yearly raise is only in line with inflation instead of above it, try to sit down with your boss to discuss the issue. If you're a business owner, consider it acceptable to raise your prices slightly.

I'm no inflation guru, but I know enough to keep a steady head and to stay ahead of it.

Here is a fun example that is most likely the reality for many people around the ages of 50-60, maybe up to 65, in the States.

You started working at a company in 2000. With the little experience that you had at the time, you got a great job working in administration that paid $15/hour. Yes! With minimum wage at around $6/hour at the time (in California), you were making gold. Cool.

Year after year, you were an amazing employee, always hitting your goals, even exceeding expectations on a regular basis. Your bosses were always impressed. Whereas you were never interested in moving into a management position, which would have required you to learn a new set of social skills and take on more responsibilities, you were still granted some raises as time went on.

With an average of a 50-cent increase per hour for 22 years, after those 22 years, you were now making $26/hour. Wow! That's a 43 percent wage increase!

Okay, wait. But because inflation grew at an average of 2.11 percent per year from 2000 to 2022, the purchasing power of $15 is now equivalent to $24.71. Meaning that if you were to buy a shirt for $15 in 2000, it would now cost $24.71, assuming it kept up with inflation at an identical rate.

To say that you are earning *the same* income now as you were in 2000, you would need to be making a minimum of $24.71 per hour in order to be able to buy the same things you would have bought in the past.

In this example, however, a 43 percent increase in the brute number left you at $26, a mere $1.29 more than adjusted price for increased living costs. Your only raise over 22 years of hard work is equivalent to one-dollar-and-twenty-nine-cents of the US dollar per hour in 2022.

Now let's take into consideration that the price for everything else has gone up.

For making numbers basic, health insurance, which used to cost $100, now costs $150 per month. Need new glasses every two years? Those cost more. Gas? Right now, it's up to $6/gallon, which is unheard of in the States. Food? Double the price. Education? Don't get me started. And your salary hasn't grown essentially at all in the first quarter of the new century. Where am I going with all this?

One, I'm extremely interested in finances.

Two, switching jobs allowed me to get way ahead of inflation and gave me a stable base with extra money to start investing sooner rather than later, which will put me financially ahead of other people down the line.

I always had enough cash on hand to last me three to six months without working, in the worst-case scenario. I'm opening a private long-term life insurance plan with living benefits. Life insurance is typically for when you're married and have kids and want them to be protected in the case that you (God forbid) die, but I use it as a growing account for my future. With the living benefits feature, if I am diagnosed with any terminal illness that makes it impossible for me to complete two of seven daily functions, then I get a monthly paycheck from them. It earns interest at the same rate of inflation each year and compounds, meaning I earn interest on my interest, not just the principal balance. Since I am signed up for a permanent life insurance plan rather than a temporary one, once I am at retirement age, I'm allowed to take out any of the money in my account (principal or interest earned) without paying taxes or fees on it. Free money when I'm older? Yes please! And it all kept up with inflation. I also have a Roth IRA account (feel free to google the difference between Roth and non-Roth accounts) and an annuity opening up.

I must admit, it was a little more difficult for me to open up a life insurance account because of being bipolar. It's considered a strong negative factor in the application. I was rejected from National Life and was quoted $100 more per month for a non-profit life insurance company because I was considered higher risk. I had too many troubles with Nationwide, so I ended up losing the $100 application fee. I didn't give up, though. I understand the importance of having the account open and running from a younger age.

I also have some stocks I purchased through Interactive Brokers. This platform was best for me because of my tendency to be in different countries all the time. There are great other platforms and applications, though, including Robinhood, that I recommend. This requires you to be physically residing in the US, which was not necessarily in my plans.

There are only three platforms I know of that allow for investing for US citizens while residing outside US borders. (They check your IP address every time you log in. Believe me, I know.)

I tried Robinhood, Acorn, some banks, and nothing allowed me to legally invest while residing or traveling to other countries. You can try to use an IP switch app on your phone or computer to simulate being back in the States, but honestly, I highly recommend just doing things the legal way.

Maybe finances aren't as interesting to you as they are to me, but understanding myself enough to know that I can get bored and quit a job essentially at any moment, I want to have the freedom financially and mental tranquility to be able to do so.

That means having my three to six months of salary saved up for emergency use and a long-term plan that will cover me when I am old and even wackier than I am now.

And although I never went into this topic specifically, stay out of credit card debt. Google it. Talk to a financial advisor. Whatever you need to do. Just stop swiping unless you can fully pay it off in cash that month.

How is bipolar my superpower here? Being proactive and self-reflective, I knew and know that I would and will have ups and downs, so I set up automatic investments, payments, and other accounts so that I would not have to think of it. Also, switching jobs frequently gave me more exposure and greater income than other people of my same age. The fear and insecurity I felt emotionally, encouraged and pushed me to set up external barriers that will protect me in the future. Without bipolar, I can assume that I would have gone through the world thinking that things will stay more or less the same and that there is no reason to think too much about the future. I am *acutely* aware that things will change because of both my own doing and changes from my environment. I'm thankful that bipolarity gave me the awareness early on so that I could plan accordingly.

CHAPTER 11

How to Interact with Your Bipolar Friend or Family Member

We're weird, I know.

A little moody, a little all over the place. Super secure sometimes and super not at others.

It can be a headache for you. It's a headache for me.

Sometimes, it leads to the best stories of your life; sometimes, you'd rather punch your friend in the mouth.

Sometimes we bipolar individuals plan out an entire project with so much detail, it seems there is absolutely no way it could fail. The next day, we have to share that the concept was wrong from the beginning.

Don't be scared. Don't be intimidated. We're just normal people. ;)

The first tip I can suggest is to not treat us like extremely different people.

"Are you feeling bipolar today?"

"Have you had a mood swing lately?"

"Are you depressed?"

These are examples of questions to not ask your bipolar friend or family member unless you have received explicit verbal confirmation that you are at a point in the friendship where such questions are valued rather than intrusive.

For parents, it would be best to assume that you are not in

that comfort zone with your child. Every child hides things from his or her parents. Although I can see how technically it would be beneficial for kids to share this information with their parents, they don't. So don't barge into their emotional room without consent. Verbal consent. And you may have to check in once in a while to ensure that your bipolar child is comfortable with your questions, because opinions can change over time.

Instead of the question above, ask simpler questions such as:
"How are you feeling today?"
"Anything interesting going on in your life?"
"Tell me about your week."

These are general questions. If the bipolar individual wants to share more details about his or her current situation, then be an open ear. Since your friend/family member was confident enough in the relationship to share with you that he/she is bipolar, be grateful and don't push more than necessary.

Tip number two for friends of bipolar people: stop giving suggestions. As mentioned above, be an open ear...*and a closed mouth*. Honestly, I believe this can extend to so much more than just bipolar individuals. Most people just want to be heard and not told how to feel.

Unless the person explicitly stated that you should check up on them, then understand that you are not his or her prescribed doctor, mental health advisor, or anyone else with authority over their decisions.

The only reason you should be getting involved is if his or her life is in danger. In which case, yes, of course; call 911 if it's an emergency or get in contact with a local mental health clinic. Most clinics have a system in place where you can call to anonymously report someone who may need help. The clinic will then reach out to the individual and take it professionally from there. Some people may need help with that first step for fear of speaking to a certified mental health specialist, so the clinic reaching out helps. Remember, it's not your place to fix any problem unless *specifically* asked to do so.

Don't go rummaging through his or her medicine or alcohol cabinet to figure out if they are medicating correctly or drinking more alcohol than they should. (My mom went through my medicine cabinet in college to find my prescription drugs, and needless to say, I'm still scarred by that incident. I wasn't ready to talk about it, and her forcing me out of my shell did more harm than good.)

Again, you're not the expert. You are there to be a supportive post.

Close your mouth. Open your ears. Don't go poking around.

Respond by asking for more clarity or just opening the space to vent more.

"Oh, I've never felt that way before, could you explain it more."

"That sucks. You must feel horrible. Keep talking."

"Wow, I'm so glad you finished all of this! I'm sure your project will be amazing. Keep me updated on the progress."

Please, never equate their worth to bipolarity.

"Oh, you're probably doing that just because you're on a high right now."

It's like saying "oh, you're only smart because you have a big nose." As if people with small noses can't be smart.

(Notice correlation with racism. Any skin tone can do anything. It would behoove us all to not judge the level of melatonin and give each person a working chance not based on something they were born with and couldn't control.)

Tip three: regularly check in just to say hi.

My experience with feeling lonely was because I simply had no one who said hi.

Even something as simple as "I was thinking of you and thought to say hi" via text or DM is probably your best bet.

Tip four: Assume that every bipolar person is different.

If you know more than one bipolar person, you probably noticed that they experience different symptoms.

Bipolar is not like when women living together end up matching their period cycles. Two bipolar individuals won't go through manic and depressive episodes together.

My college roommate got seasonal depression, which is also different and not reliant on the cycle of someone else, but rather the time of year.

I can suggest not responding with comments like:

"Oh, I know how it is because my other friend had the same thing."

"My other friend just did X, and they got over it."

"That's not as bad as what my friend described; you'll be fine."

Instead, try saying things like:

"Interesting. I previously thought that those emotions only manifest one way. Your situation seems unique. Give me more detail."

"Someone else I know has similar tendencies, but I'm interested to know how you experience them and react."

"That's a tough situation." Then be quiet. Sit and let your friend continue to vent.

Note: Even if you *think* you know the right answer or solution to the situation, just let your friend or family member talk. Your opinion will be fully valued when asked for.

If you're dyyyyiiinnngggg to share, you might try politely stating, "I know you're using this time to vent, and I want to provide a safe space for you. I might have a solution but don't want to give unsolicited advice without asking permission first. Would you want my opinion, or are you just sharing your feelings?"

You have to be okay with them asking for you to keep your suggestions out. However, if they open the doors, feel free to share what's on your mind.

Tip five: Bipolar people have been called crazy enough; you don't have to add on.

Unless you are just saying they are crazy in a friendly way or you are close enough to have the confidence to say they are crazy, I would shy away from anything related to that.

Honestly, we know.

We friggin know.

Some people are perhaps more aware than others about when exactly his or her actions are not in line with society's norms, but in general, we know we're a little off.

I know when I want to sit on the shower floor for half an hour and do nothing. I also know when I want to be in the sun all day long without coming home for what seems like forever.

I also know when I wake up at 3:24 AM with the need to research horses ASAP, I'm probably not completely in line with what a non-bipolar person would be doing.

I hope this was able to help a little bit with understanding best practices when interacting with a bipolar person!

CONCLUSION

I've been working on this book for years and just now I decided to google "positive traits in bipolar people."

The past four months that I've spent refining my writing and actually forming the book, I was constantly driving to find the positive at the end of every section to show how bipolarity is my superpower. I never thought to google it for comparison with what other people think.

The first positive psychological trait that came up was "resilience." I love it. A study by Karger in 2016 found that most bipolar people demonstrate the characteristic of resilience.

This same study states: "Western cultural notions of 'mad geniuses' and 'artistic temperaments' date back to Aristotle's observation that 'no great genius has ever existed without a strain of madness'" (Motto). I also like that. I'm a little crazy but also a little genius, thank you very much.

For reasons similar to what I have explained throughout the length of this book, I have had no other choice than to learn how to deal with my emotions.

They aren't going away, and whereas the frequency, gravity, and intensity may change over the span of my life, I will still get manic and depressive episodes. I'll just have to deal with that and learn how to best use what was given to me to come out on top.

Some of the first pages on Google also touched on creativity. Creativity isn't a standard across the block for everyone diagnosed with bipolar, according to the articles that I read.

I feel that creativity is such a hard term to define or even measure. I used to not think I was creative because I couldn't draw and really didn't care either. It doesn't calm me or even entertain me.

However, I love to dance and decorate my room. Those activities can definitely be considered creative. I also enjoy writing, so that can be creative. And I've learned to absolutely love sales. Sales is so much more creative than people would think—learning how to interact with other people and then designing a contract that is in line with everything that they want and that you can offer. I love it. And I always try to get my clients exactly what they want. Sometimes messing with the terms a little bit can provide the right amount of flexibility that will get a potential client over the line to sign.

Another positive trait is that, from a young age, I was obligated to not put myself above my biology. Huh? Let me explain.

I read lots of self-help and leadership books.

Author after author relays the importance of getting seven and a half to eight hours of sleep every single night. Also, drink lots of water, workout every day, give yourself alone time but also go on nature hikes once in a while.

No one is superhuman. You are not above your biology. You can't choose to not eat for a week and expect to be fine and dandy, unless you are an avid faster in which case you might be used to it. You can't pull an all-nighter and expect your brain function to be at top performance level. You can't expect to not work out and have healthy internal systems (notice I don't mention the physical aspect. That's just a bonus).

Your basic necessities need to be met before you can think about being successful elsewhere.

Maslow's hierarchy of needs is a perfect representation of exactly this.

Maslow was an American psychologist who created a triangular visual representation of the physiological traits that human beings need to adhere to prior to expecting success in any other field of his or her life.

Maslow extended his explanation of the hierarchy explaining that in lieu of treating an individual as a "bag of symptoms," health professionals or even the individual should focus on aspects separately, but in a certain order.

The order is as follows and starts with the basic physical needs and increases to the basic emotional needs:
1. Physiological needs: Food, water, sleep, movement
2. Safety needs: Security
3. Belongingness and love needs: Intimate relationships, family and friends
4. Esteem needs: Feeling of accomplishment and success
5. Self-actualization: Achieving one's full potential, content with oneself

Many people do not have to deal with looking at charts or explanations like this until they are in their forties or fifties and have to deal with the fact that they don't like where they are in life, are too stressed out and realize they haven't been taking care of themselves first.

In order to be successful in whatever your personal definition of success may be, you need to take care of yourself first.

Feed yourself with healthy food but also with a good amount of knowledge that will allow you to grow to new levels.

I, and other individuals who deal with any sort of mental disorder from a younger age, was forced to grapple with this idea early on. I couldn't function without eight hours of sleep. As a high school senior, varsity cheer captain, IB full diploma candidate, applying to college, etc., I got eight hours of sleep every night. Looking back, I still have no idea how I did it, but time management was extremely important to me and still is.

Fast forward a few years, as a college senior, I was taking 20-unit semesters (normal was 16) and working three part-time jobs, one of which was the opening shift at the library (6:00 AM clock-in time, Monday through Friday). I still got eight hours of sleep, ate well enough for a college student, and worked out every day. (I was very close to having no money, but that's a different story).

Since I lived with 12 people, I must say my social life was still existent. Hot tip for anyone that likes to stay home but also be social, get roommates. And I still went out on weekends.

I read a quoted conversation once that changed my perspective of the rich versus the poor. I can't remember who said it, but it goes something like this:

- "How many hours do you have in a day?"
- "Twenty-four."
- "How many hours does [insert rich person's name of choice] have in his/her day?"
- "Twenty-four."
- "So what are you doing with your time that is different from [insert rich person's name from above]?"

That moved me. It's true. I can't go above my biology, meaning I definitely can't go above nature either. I am given a new 24 hours each day, and so is everyone else, rich or poor, successful or not. How I choose to structure those 24 hours is up to me. I can be reading on a business topic, which will help me advance future endeavors, or I can sit down with a glass of wine and watch a chick flick (I find this super necessary sometimes, but not every day or every week). I can choose to be strategizing for my side businesses, or I can go shopping and frivolously spend my money on a new lotion from Victoria's Secret and a cute new dress I didn't need.

I am bipolar and had to find the best ways for me to work at first in line with everyone else and later in line with my own morals and greater goals.

Reading all my mentality books and self-help books, I realized that I already had an advantage over others who were just starting on their journey of organizing their life.

Bipolar was and is my superpower.

Not knowing I had bipolar disorder sucked. I never knew

what was happening. It was not fun to have it hidden from me and then have to learn to deal with it later on by myself. I really did feel like there was no one who would fully support me and tell me the truth except my therapist.

However, once I started dealing with bipolar in a healthy way, I actually developed more positive skills that gave me a base for what would set me up with a great career path and strong personal morals.

Sharing my path with friends and family got easier, but I also learned to establish a base of honesty and respect before sharing. Confessing prematurely in a friendship or relationship was always a 50/50 chance that it would go well.

What I could always confirm though is that as long as I stayed true to myself, then I was happy and content. I could not and cannot pretend that my bipolarity just doesn't exist. It does. I am not above my biology, and I am not above nature. I have to use what I was given to my advantage and learn how to best interact with the negative aspects.

My intention in writing this book was to provide tools and ideas for other people with either bipolar or another mental disorder to use to their benefit. Life isn't perfect. But you can always turn a negative into a positive.

After taking you on a journey through my childhood, my pre-adult years, and my figuring-out of bipolarity, I hope that you were able to see that, although I'm different, I can still get to the outcome I want and that others achieve, just using a different method or going down a different path.

As mental illness in general gains more normalcy in society, I await the day that saying "I'm going to my therapist" is as normal as saying "I'm going to the eye doctor for a new contact lens prescription." Our brain is the most important part of our body. It's what allows us to do absolutely everything, so making sure that we are working on it, refining it, and healing it when necessary is non-negotiable for future societies.

For friends and families of bipolar individuals, I hope this book gives you more insight into how we feel. However, remember that each bipolar person is different, and the symptoms will manifest differently, meaning that you will have to ask your friend or family member what the best way to interact with *them* is. I also provided a handful of tools for you to use when interacting so as to not come off as judge-y, manipulative, or non-understanding of the situation. Overall, it's important to keep an open mind, open heart, and open opinion that what they are going through is different than what you are going through.

I continue to have ups and downs. And no doubt I will continue to grow and have a surplus more experiences to share in a few years.

But overall, I know that if I did it, then so can you!

Remember, for me bipolar is my superpower. And you can find yours, too. :)

ACKNOWLEDGEMENTS

Not one page of this book would have been written had it not been for the amazing influence of my dad. My dad is my light, my laughter, my inspiration, and my role model.

In December of 2021, I visited him in Las Vegas and we discussed goals together. The rest of December I spent detailing out my goals using the S.M.A.R.T. Goals technique. I emailed him my goals, writing a book was goal number one. He sent me back the document completely marked up in red, arguing to make my goals bigger and my timeframe more aggressive.

Because of him, this book is here today, years before I ever thought I would realistically be a published author.

Gracias, Papi, te quiero.

ABOUT THE AUTHOR

Karina Schulz was born and raised in San Diego, California to an Austrian mom and Peruvian dad. As a studious young girl and teenager, Schulz went to a German-immersion K-8 school. Then she graduated high school with the full I.B. Diploma and got accepted to the University of Southern California, where she completed her undergraduate degree in Linguistics in only three years.

She had international influence from a young age which inspired her to continue learning languages throughout her young adult life. At present, she speaks English, German, Spanish, Portuguese and Italian. She was constantly involved in sports, cheerleading and dancing being her main two interests above all. She is dedicated to being involved in and giving back to her direct communities.

One of Schulz's biggest life goals is to inspire people to learn to love themselves and to be able to successfully source the tools that they need to get to where they want to be, be in professionally or personally. This book is a direct result of that goal. Schulz realized that she was able to change her opinion of her mental state and use it to her benefit, despite society having told her otherwise. She depicts the emotional peaks and troughs that get her to where she is today and hopes that the reader will find reason to continue on his or her own path, no matter the circumstance.

Printed in the USA
CPSIA information can be obtained
at www.ICGtesting.com
LVHW050435310723
753861LV00011B/572